Heavenly Portals and the Coming Storm

A Prophetic Call from Psalm 91

*"Returning to
the Heart of the Father,
to see His manifest Glory
in troubled times."*

Linda M. Hartzell Th.D.

Table of Contents

In Appreciation

First and foremost I would like to dedicate this book to our Lord Jesus, in honor of His soon coming, with a prayer that we all may be ready to stand before Him, on that Day, as His pure and spotless Bride.

Then, I would like to honor Dr. Gwen Shaw, my spiritual mother, mentor and friend, for what has been, almost a "lifetime". Thank you for the many years of love, prayers and investing in my life. I count it an honor to have served you and served by your side all of these years.

A special thank you to Pastors Pedro and Gertrudis Ibarra, from Buenos Aires, Argentina, for your continual encouragement, prayers and support. You have been true covenant friends.

Also, thank you to so many wonderful friends who have prayed, encouraged and given their time to help during the writing of this book.

Foreword

Heavenly Portals and the Coming Storm is a
timely book. Never, have we needed Heavenly
Portals more than we do in these days, and the days
that we are speedily coming into. Men's hearts are
failing them for fear, as it says in Luke 21:26: *"Men's
hearts failing them for fear, and for looking after
those things which are coming on the earth: for the
powers of heaven shall be shaken."*

There is no doubt that the Holy Spirit has stamped
this book with His approval, because He certainly
has anointed it. You can feel God talking to you on
every single page.

I have known Linda for 28 years. She has been
a part of our staff all this time. We have had many
wonderful times together in the nations. Linda
has been my faithful interpreter into the Spanish
language, in Argentina, Spain, Central America,
Mexico, and wherever I have ministered to Spanish
speaking people. I have always appreciated the

anointing that is upon Linda, when she stands at my side, as together we have shared God's message with the people of the nations.

For many years, Linda has traveled to the nations, preaching the Word of God with great authority and unction from the Holy Spirit. It is wonderful to see how God shows up, when this gal from South Dakota ministers! It is plain to see that God is no respecter of persons. He does the same things in many of her meetings that He did for the early apostles.

I believe this book will become a best-seller, and will be translated into other languages, because it is the message of the hour. It is a confirmation of many things that God is speaking to many, who are listening to Him in the "Secret Place".

We are living in days when God is opening Heavenly Portals for His intercessors, to give them Heavenly revelations. Intercessors know things that most ordinary people don't know, because true intercessors are "Throne Room" people. They do not pray in the flesh, nor by their own understanding, but by the Holy Spirit.

When God gets ready to make a paradigm shift, He opens a portal to Heaven, like He did for Jacob at Bethel, Ezekiel in captivity, Paul on the Road to Damascus, John on the Island of Patmos, and many others. We have not only entered the day when God is doing greater signs, wonders, and miracles, but we are beginning to have access to Heavenly Portals. God is sending down to earth, new forms of worship, such as banners, dance, blowing the shofar, new anointed music and books. I believe that this book will open a Heavenly Portal for you, and bring you into a new dimension with God.

"Heavenly Portals and the Coming Storm" came from Heaven's library, and Linda was the scribe whom God chose to inscribe it in a language that we can understand.

Don't just read it, as you would read any other book, meditate on these Heavenly Truths. Pray and fast for God to open a Heavenly Portal for you.

Then, pass the good news on to others, who are hungry for more of God. Share it with those who are hungry for end-time revelations from God.

Gwen R. Shaw

President of End-Time
Handmaidens and Servants International

Psalm 91

*He that dwelleth in the secret place of the Most
High shall abide under the
shadow of the Almighty.*

*I will say of the Lord, He is my refuge and my
fortress: my God; in him will I trust.*

*Surely he shall deliver thee from the snare of the
fowler, and from the noisome pestilence.*

*He shall cover thee with his feathers, and under
his wings shalt thou trust: his truth shall be thy
shield and buckler.*

*Thou shalt not be afraid for the terror by night,
nor for the arrow that flieth by day*

*Nor for the pestilence that walketh in darkness;
nor for the destruction that wasteth at noonday.*

A thousand shall fall at thy side, and ten thousand at thy right hand; but it shall not come nigh thee.

Only with thine eyes shalt thou behold and see the reward of the wicked.

Because thou hast made the Lord, which is my refuge, even the Most High, thy habitation;

There shall no evil befall thee, neither shall any plague come nigh thy dwelling.

For he shall give his angels charge over thee, to keep thee in all thy ways.

They shall bear thee up in their hands, lest thou dash thy foot against a stone.

Thou shalt tread upon the lion and the adder: the young lion and the dragon shalt thou trample under feet.

Because he hath set his love upon me, therefore will I deliver him: I will set him on high, because he hath known my name.

He shall call upon me, and I will answer him: I will be with him in trouble: I will deliver him and honour him.

With long life will I satisfy him, and shew him my salvation.

King James Version

Introduction

"Heavenly Portals and the Coming Storm"** is a prophetic call from **Psalm 91:1**, calling God's people to come back to the heart of the Father. In this hour it is vital that we draw close to the Lord and learn His ways. He is calling us to come up higher into a new dimension of His life and love, in the shelter of His presence.

If we can learn to dwell in the Secret Place of the Most High in this hour, we will not have to be in fear and dread. We will watch the coming end-time events unfold from a whole new perspective. This perspective will be one of love and trust, as found in **Psalm 91**. We will see how God will open up heavenly portals to, His Secret Places, for blessing, provision, and protection for His people in the midst of the raging storms. (*see Psalm 91 in it's entirety).

We are entering the time known as "The Time of Jacob's Trouble" spoken of in the Bible. *"Alas for the day is great, so that none is like it: it is even the time of Jacob's trouble, but he shall be saved out of it"* **Jeremiah 30:7**

We are beginning to experience the "birth pangs" of what is getting ready to unfold in the days to come. The Dictionary definition of birth pangs is: "Incidents of disorder and distress; especially in social, moral and spiritual changes."

The Lord spoke to me recently and said: "We are coming into EXTREME times. We hear the word extreme used a lot these days: "extreme sports, "extreme adventures", "extreme makeover", extreme weather", "extreme prophetic".

The dictionary definition of the word extreme is: "of the greatest possible degree, extent or intensity, to the utmost". We have begun to see this with weather patterns, natural disasters, economic crisis, moral decline, and political agendas. Well, these are extreme days when we will need an extreme faith, grace and wisdom to meet the storms and challenges ahead. "Lukewarm" has no place in extreme times!

We will also see God manifest His greatness and Glory in extreme ways through extreme situations.

When most consider the "end-times", they can only envision it as a dark time of fear and doom. Yes, things will get more difficult, and we will have to face things that most of us have not seen or heard of in our lifetime. Nevertheless in the midst of the storms, God has a glorious plan for those who love Him and will walk in His ways.

1 Corinthians 2:9 *"Eye hath not seen, nor ear heard, neither have entered into the heart of man, the things which God hath prepared for them that love Him"* Extreme things!

This is not a time to run away and hide in a cave because of fear. It is a time to draw close to God, make sure there is nothing between you and Him. Anchor your soul in His Secret Place and prepare for the incredible, glorious things that He has in store for us! You were born for such a time as this!

Within the pages of this book you will find, what I believe, is the heartbeat of God for this hour and for our lives. You will discover:

1. An understanding of the times and the storms ahead.

2. How to not only survive but thrive in the midst of the storm.

3. How to prepare spiritually for these times.

4. How to reconnect with God's mandate for your life.

5. A vision of the outpouring of Glory that awaits us and how God will use us in His Glory.

6. What is the Secret Place? And where is it found?

7. Receiving "Secret Place" impartations that will bring transformation.

8. How we as "earthen vessels" can be used as "atmosphere changers".

9. What are "Heavenly Portals"? How God will use them in these End-Times, in our lives and around the world.

May the presence of the Lord usher you into the atmosphere of His Secret Place and may the Spirit of Wisdom, Understanding and Revelation take you, even beyond the words that are written on these pages.

"And the Spirit of the Lord shall rest upon him, the spirit of wisdom and understanding, the spirit of counsel and might, the spirit of knowledge and the fear of the Lord." **Isaiah 11:2**

Returning to the Heart
of the Father

There is a very powerful Kingdom reality in Psalm 91 for our lives. As the darkness intensifies and the storms rage on the horizon, this is the set time that God is calling us up higher to His Holy Place of abiding.

There is so much talk these days about "getting back to basics". Religion and men have made the Gospel either so complicated or so "seeker friendly" that it is losing it's relevance and authenticity for the hour that we live in. It has caused many good, dedicated Christians to become discouraged, or to walk away from traditional "Church" (as we know it).

A nationwide survey conducted by the USA based Barna Research Group shows that there are over one million Christians leaving "Church" in America every year. It is not because they are backsliding, it is because of spiritual hunger and a search for more. The greatest percentage of these

Christians remain spiritually active and committed Christians, who are in pursuit of a more fulfilling spiritual life. Many have begun to meet in home fellowships or house churches. Barna states: "This shows a historic shift in the nation's spiritual vision. It also suggests that we are on the precipice of a new era of spiritual experience and expression."[1]

There is a Divine dissatisfaction stirring in the hearts of God's people that cannot and will not be satisfied by ministry activity, "significant" others, or success. Even spiritual gifts and miracles will not suffice. Only as we return to the very heart of God will we encounter afresh, His Love and atmosphere of Glory that will fill us and flood us with the fullness of God.

Ephesians 3:17b-19 "*. . . that ye being rooted and grounded in love, may be able to comprehend with all saints what is the breadth, and length, and depth, and height; and to know the love of Christ, which passeth knowledge, that ye might be filled with all the fullness of God.*"

There is a call going forth from the Throne of God and His Holy Atmosphere for us to return to our "first love" (our first affection)

Revelation 2:4 "*Therefore, I have something against thee because thou hast left thy first love*"

As we have read and expounded on this scripture we have always put it in the context of returning to the freshness and newness of the "first love" experience we once had when we were newly saved. Although there is a truth to that, I believe that the call comes from a much deeper place and from much further back. I believe it comes from the "Womb of the Morning" **Psalm 110:3** *"Thy people shall be willing in the day of Thy power, in the beauties of holiness, from the womb of the morning"*.

This is the very heart of God where we were conceived and from whence creation came forth. It is the Secret Place of God's perfect love and holy atmosphere. This is where our spirits once abided and were accustomed to being, before we came to this earth. Our Heavenly Father, who created us, was our very first love and He is calling us to come back to His heart.

In the Secret Place we will reconnect with our true purpose and the mandate for which we were sent to this earth. We will find that Heaven itself will begin to work on our behalf. We will become "atmosphere changers" and "carriers of His Glory".

This is the very essence of *"Thy Kingdom come, Thy will be done, on earth as it is in Heaven"* **Matthew 6:10**

The Secret Place

As we look at the words "Secret Place" a little closer in the original Greek, we see a greater depth of meaning.

Secret Place = "a covering, hidden place of protection, council, intimacy, private, inward, a place where treasures are kept".

In this book we will look at three dimensions of the "Secret Place" that are mentioned in scripture. We will discover the secret place of the enemy, the secret place of our soul, and the Secret Place of the Most High.

The Enemy Has a Secret Place

Psalm 10:8-9 *"He sitteth in the lurking places of the villages, in the secret places doth he murder the innocent, his eyes are privily set against the poor"*

Evil has a secret place of counsel from whence it comes. It is conceived and sustained behind a veil of darkness. Evil seeks the darkness, and to be hidden, as to catch one "unawares". It does not like the light or to be discovered. This is why at times evil has had the power to prevail. This is why at times criminals have not been able to be found. They operate behind a cloak of darkness.

The scripture says in **II Corinthians 4:3-4** *"But if our Gospel be hid, it is hid from them that are lost; in whom the "god of this world" hath blinded the minds of them that believe not, lest the light of the glorious gospel of Christ, who is the image of God should shine unto them"*

Even though for a season satan operates as "god of this world", God Almighty remains King over all the earth! **Psalm 47:7** *"For God is King over all the earth. Sing ye praises with understanding."*

It would seem from looking at the words "world" and "earth" that they would probably have the same meaning. But as I began to look a little deeper into the Greek and Hebrew, I found that the original context of these two words bring out a noted difference. The word "world" infers: "Fleeting, portion of time, wilderness, world as transient, **spirit of the age,** habitants as those subject to the spirit of the world."

The word "earth" has a much different meaning. "Earth" is defined as land, nations, regions, globe, clay, earthen vessels.

1 Corinthians 10:26 *says: "For the earth is the Lord's and the fullness thereof"*

In **Isaiah 60:1-2** *it says: "Arise, shine, for thy light is come, and the Glory of the Lord is risen upon thee. For behold the darkness shall cover the earth and gross darkness the people: but the Lord shall arise upon thee, and His Glory shall be seen upon thee"*

Even though we are coming into days of darkness and great trial, the light remains the same, "LIGHT". Light always shines brighter in the darkness. Darkness can never extinguish the light, it will only enhance it!

If you are a worshiper and a lover of Jesus Christ, you need not fear the growing darkness. Just continue steadfast to be who you are. As the darkness increases, the light of Christ within you will shine brighter and brighter unto that coming day. The Glory of the Lord shall rise upon you!

The Secret Place of the Soul

God has created in each individual a "secret place", also known as our soul.

The dictionary definition of the soul is: "The immaterial part of a person, the actuating cause of an individual life which concerns life, action and emotion, while the spirit is related to worship and divine communion."

The soul is the secret place of free will and personality. It is the meeting place that brings union between the body and spirit. Through the body the soul relates to the world around him, to influence and to be influenced by it.

Through the spirit we relate to God and the spiritual world. We receive of the life and power of God. When our soul is yielded to the spirit, we become a channel for God to use us to touch humanity.

So, in truth our soul stands between two worlds, but belonging to both. Through Jesus Christ, the "life giving Spirit" we can stand rightly related to God, to be that intermediary (intercessor) between God and man. Thus being a portal (doorway) for God's presence and power to move upon the earth.

Thus, we see that through the power of the soul, man does influence his surroundings for good or evil. The soul has it's own power to determine it's path of influence [2]

God respects the sanctity and dignity of each soul to make it's own moral choices. This secret place is meant to be and should be kept as a Holy Sanctuary for the presence of the Lord, a place reserved for inspiration and revelation. But many times, even in the lives of Christians, this place becomes a "seed bed" of bitterness, unforgivness, fear, suspicion, and lust. This secret place, is the place where sin and evil are also conceived.

James 1:14-15, *"But every man is tempted, when he is drawn away of his own lust, and enticed. Then when lust has conceived, it bringeth forth sin, when it is finished bringeth forth death."*

The Power and Potential of the Soul

In the beginning God created Adam a "living soul" as it says in **Genesis 2:7** *"And the Lord God formed man of the dust of the ground, and breathed into his nostrils the breath of life; and man became a living soul."*

Adam was the finest specimen of a man that ever walked this earth. He was vibrant, strong and healthy. Adam communed with God and his soul was quickened to a higher life by the Glory of God. This Glory (God ability) quickened his senses, his potentials, his gifting and skills in everything he did. Adam was created in the Holy Atmosphere of God's Glory; and he was accustomed to living there.

When Adam and Eve disobeyed God and partook of the tree of the "knowledge of good and evil", their Holy innocence was gone and they knew that they were naked. That vital connection with God's Glory had been broken, and a spiritual death process began. They were afraid and sought to hide from the very Presence that once enveloped their lives and made them the glorious beings that they were.

That higher dimension of their soul that connected with the supernatural was shut down and the flesh took dominion. Thus the latent power (potential) of the soul was locked in flesh. It is said that today man only uses between 1% to 10% of the potential brain power for which he was created to use.

Man was created for the "extra ordinary", for the supernatural, for the challenge of seeing things made possible in the realm of impossibilities. To this day man seeks through many ways and many forms to reconnect with the realm of the supernatural, so that his soul may once again ascend to that higher place of "super-human" abilities.

In the Hindu, Buddhist and other religions they make great sacrifices of fasting and ascetic lifestyles to breakdown the dominion of the flesh, that the soul may be released to ascend to a higher place. Yes, they are even known to see "supernatural" activity and healings in their midst. This is the power of the soul. But, when their soul ascends it is entering a supernatural realm of darkness that opens the door to demonic spiritual activity from the second heaven. The soul and the devil can "mimic" the things of the Holy Spirit.

The gift of God is free but the way of darkness has a very high eternal price tag attached. It is the price of your soul.

It is only through Jesus Christ, the second Adam, whom God created a "quickening" or "life giving Spirit' that we can lawfully reconnect and ascend to that higher life of God's Glory and supernatural ability.

1 Corinthians 15:45 *". . . The first man Adam was made a "living soul"; the last Adam was made a "quickening Spirit".*

The Scripture in **1 Thessalonians 5:23** shows us that God has created us a "triune" or three part being, spirit, soul and body. *"And the very God of peace sanctify you wholly; and I pray God, your whole spirit and soul and body be preserved blameless unto the coming of our Lord Jesus Christ."*
The spirit is God given, the soul is God breathed, and the body is God formed.

Clearing of the Soul

The Lord says He requires truth in the inward parts. **Psalm 51:6** *"Behold thou desirest truth in the inward parts: and in the hidden part Thou shalt make me to know wisdom."*
God is calling for truth in every area of our lives, even in the deepest, most intimate part of our being. We must desire truth and to be true to ourselves and true to God. Because it is the truth that will set us free. **John 8:32** *"And ye shall know the truth and the truth shall make you free".*
Truth is a fruit of the secret place. We are only as free, as holy or as true as what we are in secret. It is not what is done in open that determines who we are. It is what we do, and what we contemplate in secret when no one is watching. What does your

28

secret place consist of? What rules there? What are your meditations and desires there? What you are in secret today will be manifest tomorrow. "As a man thinketh, so is he."

Proverbs 4:23 *says "Keep thy heart with all diligence; for out of it are the issues of life."*

your Soul

Your soul is the deepest, innermost part of you. It is the very core of your being. It is the center of your strength or your weakness. It is the center of your spirituality or your carnality. It is the place of contemplation and meditation where the seed of vision or the seed of sin is produced and conceived. The soul is a fountain of life where we give from and where we receive.

When we come to Jesus, we are made holy in innocence by the Blood of Jesus. But we are only made holy in character by a series of moral choices that begin in the secret place of our soul.

Psalm 119:11 *says "Thy Word have I hid in mine heart, that I might not sin against thee."*

Depending on how we keep our heart, what we feed on and where we allow it to wander will determine the path that our soul and eventually our lives will take.

29

If you entertain thoughts of anger, offence or suspicion it will lead to bitterness of soul and self destruction.

If you allow lust to take root it will open the door to demonic strongholds that will torment and destroy the moral fiber of your being, and bring brokenness and pain to you and your family.

If you embrace the ideals of any thought process that leads you away from the truth of the Word of God, it will produce a "toxic" mixture in your soul. This will produce confusion and strife and lead you down a dead-end path that you really do not want to go!

All roads do not lead to God. Jesus said: *"I am the Way, the Truth and the Life. . . .No man comes to the Father but by Me."* **John 14:6**

We cannot pick and choose the thought processes that appeal to us to create our own belief system. Truth is not relative, according to what we perceive it to be. There must be an absolute. The Word of God is an absolute that has been proven over the centuries of time to be faithful and true. Only the Word of God will strengthen, establish and settle your soul in the storms of life and in eternal matters.

1 Peter 5:10 *says: "But the God of all grace; who hath called us unto His eternal glory by Christ Jesus, after that you have suffered awhile, make you perfect, stablish, strengthen, settle you."*

It has been proven that 97% of what forms us and influences our character and personality is our environment. Only 3% is genetic. We may not be able to control all of our environment, but the environment of our personal soul we can control.

"Finally brethren, whatsoever things are true, whatsoever things are honest, whatsoever things are just, whatsoever things are pure, whatsoever things are lovely, whatsoever things are of a good report; if there be any virtue, and if there be any praise, think on these things." **Philippians 4:8**

Sanctify the secret place of your soul. Make way for the Lord to reign there. Prepare a sanctuary for the time of storm.

Cycles of the Soul

Just as God has set the universe in motion by cycles (solar cycles, lunar cycles, spring, winter, summer, fall, seed time and harvest etc…), so our lives go through cycles.

Many times cycles are set in motion in our lives by choices we make that produce consequences either for good and for blessing, or for defeat and sorrow.

When the Word of God is alive in our heart and we choose to walk in the Spirit and sow to the Spirit, we shall reap the life of the Spirit. It is always a path of blessing and joy.

Then there are cycles of our soul that are set in motion by erroneous belief systems, habits, conditioned responses or behavioral patterns, that produce negative consequences in our life. They hinder us from occupying our place of victory or breakthrough.

It is one thing to receive a breakthrough, but it is another thing to occupy that place of breakthrough. We must learn to be able to maintain our open heaven or victory, and walk out our blessing.

We can desire change and pray for breakthrough. God can give us "seasons" of victory. During these seasons we begin to step into something new in God and enjoy the blessings and presence of the Lord for a time. However, as soon as opposition arises, old, familiar behavioral patterns or conditioned responses arise and we revert back to old ways and habits. When we do, we step out of our "open heaven' and begin another cycle of the same old struggles and problems. When this happens we never seem to fully "occupy" or "own" our place of breakthrough. Thus we become disillusioned and wonder where God is. Remember it is you that has moved, not God. God in this season wants to deliver us to the utmost, so that we will be completely free from things that have hindered and bound us for many years and some even for a lifetime.

Cycles are costly. They can cause discouragement and depression. They can even cost opportunities, relationships and entire seasons of time in our life. Time is precious and is running out, for some faster than for others. It is time for us to come into our full stature of maturity in Christ Jesus. It is time to break out of old cycles and allow our soul to ascend to that higher life of the Spirit.

That is why it is so important that we seek God for a work of His Spirit through prayer and fasting for this season, to break out of old cycles. Fasting is a powerful key to break these cycles. Fasting is an act of surrender. Many times, we are willing to make great sacrifices for the Lord. We give our time, our energy, our finances, but all He asks for is our heart. "One cannot compensate through sacrifice for what is lost in disobedience"

There is a special grace of God in this season to break old cycles and step into a new dimension of the Spirit. A seasonal portal of God's Grace is open. God can do in our lives in five minutes of His Grace and Power what would take years of working out. Respond to His invitation. Move when He says move. Miss not your day of visitation!

There is great potential in you waiting to be unlocked, but it will only come by a **complete surrender to the Lord in the secret place of your soul.**

The Transfigured Soul

In **2 Corinthians 3:16-18** *it says: "Nevertheless when it (the heart) shall turn (yield, surrender, open) to the Lord (The Supreme Authority) the veil shall be taken away." . . . "Now the Lord is that Spirit:*

33

*and where the Spirit of the Lord (The Supreme Authority) is, there is liberty. But we all with open face beholding as in a glass the glory of the Lord, are changed (transfigured, transformed) into the same image from glory to glory, even as by the Spirit of the Lord" * (KJV w/ Greek meaning in parenthesis)*

The context of verse 16 is referring to the hearts of the Jews as Moses is read unto them.(vs15) However, it is the same for us as believers, when our heart softens, yields and surrenders to the complete Lordship of the Supreme Authority. The veil shall be removed from our hearts and we shall "know" the Lord in His pure, Holy Love and Glory. This kind of encounter will change us (cause us to go through a metamorphosis) in nature and character. One cannot be touched by the true Glory of God and remain the same.

As our hearts behold Him, we shall be drawn to Him in all of His glory, splendor and love. As we shall "see" Him, we shall "know" Him and as we "know" Him we shall be changed (transfigured) into His likeness.

Psalm 17:15 *"As for me, I will behold Thy face in righteousness: I shall be satisfied when I awake in thy likeness"*

The word "changed" in the Greek is "Metamorphosis" which means to be transfigured and made into something brand new from the inside out. When the Glory of God touches our lives, we are made into something brand new and totally different, more glorious and noble than before. Like when a caterpillar is changed into a butterfly. The caterpillar is changed from an "earthy", earth bound crawling creature, into a beautiful, colorful, airborne creature without the "earthy" limitation.

In **1 Corinthians 15: 47-49** *it says: "The first man (Adam) is of the earth, "earthy": the second man (Jesus) is the Lord from heaven. As is the earthy, such are they also they that are earthy: and as is the heavenly, such are they also that are heavenly. And as we have borne the image of the earthy, we shall also bear the image of the heavenly."*

It is interesting to follow the stages of the metamorphosis of the Monarch Butterfly. The Monarch is one of the biggest, strongest and most beautiful of it's species. It even has been known to travel between continents. When the caterpillar (larvae) is hatched, it's egg had already strategically been placed on the Milk Thistle Foliage. This is the best kind for it's species and it's particular growth process and nourishment. The caterpillar will feed on this foliage until it is fully grown. The time will come when the caterpillar will outgrow the need for this and will begin to separate itself, seeking a place where it can "pupate" or shed it's skin and begin the process of "cocooning" It instinctively knows that it must go through this process before it can begin it's next stage of life. It then begins a process of surrender and leaving behind the old life as it sheds it's skin and begins to be enclosed in the cocoon for a season of time, alone. Interestingly, inherent within each caterpillar is what it needs to become a butterfly. After the encounter in the cocoon the caterpillar emerges into a new life and a new way of life. It even has a new name: Butterfly.[3]

So we have come to a time that even the greatest of what we have known in our Christian experience and ministry will not be enough to sustain us in the days ahead. It is time for a fresh consecration and surrender. It is time to break through the veil and come away into the secret, hidden place, in the Presence of the Lord where we can behold Him in His Glory. It is a place where we must go alone to have a personal encounter with Christ. It is a place where we must leave behind our old life to receive His new, resurrection life. Here we will find our true identity in Christ. When we discover our identity in Him we can then reconnect with the mandate for which we were sent to this earth. Too, often a person has identity in what they do, such as mother, teacher, preacher, wife etc. instead of who they are in Christ. Inherent within us is what we need for this transfiguration. It is *"Christ in you, the hope of Glory"* **Colossians 1:27b**

Many times it is divine desperation that will drive us to this place of encounter. Maybe you have come to a place and time that you feel you are at a dead-end street, and there is no going back. You may be experiencing the pain and shame of weakness or failure. Maybe it is a time where your friends or family have forsaken you, or a time of great betrayal. You may have become disillusioned with religion, or other Christians. You may be broken, and at a place where the tears do not cease to flow. Words may not even be sufficient to express what you are experiencing. Just run into the arms of Jesus and He will draw you into His secret place. There He will comfort you and counsel you and heal you. He will give you new life, resurrection life. He will give you joy for your sorrow, beauty for your ashes, and glory for your affliction. You may even have to wrestle with the angel, as Jacob did, alone, to receive the blessing of the Lord and your new name.

Genesis 32:24-28 *"And Jacob was left alone; and there wrestled a man with him until the breaking of the day. And when he saw that he prevailed not against him, he touched the hollow of his thigh; and the hollow of Jacob's thigh was out of joint, and he wrestled with him. And he said let me go, for the day breaketh. And he said I will not let thee go, except thou bless me. And he said, what is thy name? And he said Jacob. And he said thy name shall be called* *no more Jacob, but Israel: for as a prince hast thou power with God and with men, and hast prevailed."*

When you emerge from your secret place of encounter, you shall emerge with new life, and a new name before God. You will be able to fly to new heights, and to new nations. You will find that the earthly, carnal things will not have the power to hold, you as they once did.

Through the Blood of Jesus we have been made new creatures in Christ Jesus. It is time for us to come into the revelation of our full redemption, and the Glory that He has called us to be reconciled to.

Even Jesus, who was accustomed to communing closely with the Father, was transfigured when the Glory of God came upon Him. **Matthew 17:2** *"and (Jesus) was transfigured before them: and His face did shine as the sun, and His raiment was as white as light"*

Glorious Light in Earthen Vessels

"For God who commanded the light to shine out of darkness, hath shined in our hearts, to give the light of the knowledge of the Glory of God in the face of Jesus Christ. But we have this treasure in earthen vessels, that the excellency of the power may be of God and not of us." **2 Corinthians 4:6-7**

When we are touched by glory and the work of the Holy Spirit begins to change us, the excellency of God's Glory will begin to shine out from us. There are varying degrees of light and distinct clarity of brilliance. As we press on to know the Lord we will be changed from glory to glory into a vessel of honor.

In Bible times and even in many nations to this day, when someone searches to buy quality pottery that will be durable for extreme use, it is held up to the light.[4] If the vessel is found to be whole, and without flaw, it is called a "sincere vessel", (pure, genuine, without deceit). One of the Greek definitions for "sincere" is: "judged by light". The light will also reveal if there are cracks, fissures or cosmetic "cover-ups". These vessels can be used for adornment but when they are put to the first extreme test they will leak or crumble because of the stress.

We have seen what happens in the lives of men and women of God who walk in an anointing, but their personal lives and characters go unchecked using a cosmetic "cover-up" for character flaws, moral failure and emotional weakness. Their vessel and ministry eventually crumble under the stress. The continued anointing and "blessing" is not always a sign that everything is alright in a life or ministry. It is just a matter of time until the burden of the error will break the vessel.

Spiritual erosion in the foundation of any building weakens the structure but cannot always be detected by appearance. Never be in a hurry to push to promote yourself or grow your ministry. You may be creating something that your foundation is not ready to sustain. It is not always about gifting, or anointing, or other people's accolades. The Lord Himself will promote you in His time. Be true to yourself and to God, for the sake of His honor and for your future. May your name always give honor to the Lord.

Psalm 51:6 says: *"Behold thou desirest truth in the inward parts: and in the hidden part thou shalt make me to know wisdom."*

Allow the searchlight of the Holy Spirit to search out your hidden parts. There is great grace in this season for repentance, healing, deliverance, and restoration regarding our character and inner life. Only holiness will be able to sustain the weight of the test of this hour and the Glory God wants to give us. Prepare to be a vessel of His Glory.

This is a very real encounter that He is calling us to. It is not something that can be understood or achieved with the mind. It is a heart issue. It is one of responding to the divine workings of the Holy Spirit in our lives.

"Many questions need no answers, for when our heart is one with the Father, understanding becomes an illumination of the heart, and not an achievement of the mind." Seek to be one with the Father through loving Him. Pure, unselfish love will draw you to His heart and bring understanding.

The Lord is searching to and fro throughout the earth among the hearts of those who are called by His name. He is looking for those that will turn to Him with all of their hearts in yielded surrender.

As you stand before Him with every pretense stripped away in loving surrender, you will see that the veil over your heart will be pulled away and the Glory of the Lord will have a divine entrance into your life. Jesus will stamp His image upon you. You will begin to reflect His countenance and carry His fragrance wherever you go.

Moses in the Mount of God

Exodus 24:15-18 *"Moses went up into the mount, and a cloud covered the mount. And the Glory of the Lord abode upon Mt. Sinai, and the cloud covered it six days: and the seventh day He called unto Moses out of the midst of the cloud. And the sight of the glory of the Lord was like devouring fire on top of the mount in the eyes of the children of Israel. And Moses went into the midst of the cloud, and gat him up into the mount: and Moses was in the mount 40 days and 40 nights."*

We see in this account of Scripture that God called Moses up into His Glory to commune with Him on Mt. Sinai. During this encounter in God's Glory, God wrote the 10 commandments with His own finger and delivered them into the hands of Moses for the direction, blessing, and well being of the Children of Israel. Also, during this time of communing in the Glory, God had a very detailed discourse with Moses, giving the blueprint for the tabernacle so that God Himself (His Glory) could come down and dwell among men. **Exodus chapter 25-31** gives us a very detailed account of this.

In waiting for Moses, the Children of Israel became impatient and felt they must take things into their own hands. They took the very offerings of gold that were to be consecrated, holy, unto the Lord for the preparation of the tabernacle and began to fashion another "god" to worship. It was all done in the name of Jehovah.

It says in **Exodus 32:5** *"And when Aaron saw it* (the golden calf), *he built an altar before it: and Aaron made proclamation, and said, tomorrow is a feast to the **Lord**"*

The interesting thing is that the word for Lord here in Hebrew, means: "the name for Jehovah, the One Supreme God". Was Aaron presuming that what they had done would be acceptable in the eyes of the Lord God Jehovah?

How many times instead of paying the price to wait upon the Lord for His direction and blueprint that will bring His Glory and highest blessing, are things taken into peoples own hands?

Great plans and ambitions are brought about. Sermons are preached that will not "offend" anyone. Instead of pure worship from Holy vessels who have prepared themselves in prayer and fasting, there are talented musicians living in sin, presuming to carry the Ark of the Lord's presence. "All inclusive" doctrines are being introduced proclaiming that all worship "one" God, no matter what His name is; Jesus, Ala, Buddha, or any of the numerous Hindu gods, all for the sake of tolerance and unity. One cannot legislate true unity. It is the work of the Holy Spirit in the heart of the true believer. These things are all "a form of godliness denying the power thereof"

2 Timothy 3:5 *"Having a form of godliness, but denying the power thereof, from such turn away."*

This is not the path to God's Glory. God has a pattern. God has a plan for all peoples and all nations. If we will follow His pattern, He will lead us into His Glory. Our lives will prosper and be blessed.

Glory

Because of the great emphasis on the Glory of God awaiting us, I want to expound on the essence of what the Glory of God is. Oh, for the human heart to try and portray the Glory of God!

The Bible dictionary definition for Glory is: God's intrinsic weightiness or greatness, His manifold majesty, brilliance, depth, awesomeness.

The Hebrew word for Glory is: (Kabod) which means a weight related with a physical phenomena in which the Presence of God is made known. It is also associated with His character and righteousness.

The Aramaic definition for Glory is: rare brightness, light, beauty, desirable, the external, physical manifestation of preeminence, majesty and dignity.

My definition of Glory is: The essence and sovereign manifestation of God, the atmosphere and "oxygen" of Heaven.

Many times the manifestation of Glory will be a weighty, tangible presence of God, accompanied by a mist or thick cloud in the atmosphere, pillars or tongues of fire, brilliant light, or golden hues.

Anointing is very different from the Glory. Anointing is an empowering for ministry, a working of the Holy Spirit in and through our lives. The anointing abides on one's life as a seal of God, for service, confirming their call.

The Glory of God is a sovereign expression and manifestation of God Himself. There are times when the Glory of God will work with the anointing or with an anointed vessel, to bring supernatural manifestations and encounters into peoples lives. Always after an encounter with true Glory the life is changed and will never be the same again.

Many times, when we experience the presence of the Lord, or a moving of the Holy Spirit in our midst, there is great blessing and rejoicing for the moment. But many go away from the experience, never seeming to be changed.

Many times the Glory clouds come and go without yielding rain, because God's people have not learned the ways of the Glory. The more we come to know the ways of the Glory, the more we will understand how to access the power of the Glory.

We have learned to approach His presence to be pacified, soothed, comforted, and ministered to, but have stopped short of pressing through to the Glory that burns and transforms. The Presence brings blessing and refreshing but the Glory shakes and brings change. The Presence is a promise but the

Glory is a privilege with a price. It is obtained at a great price through extreme circumstances.

Also, when God sends His ministering angels from the realms of Glory, to work with us and on our behalf, they will come carrying the essence of Glory. Angels inhabit the atmosphere of heaven. They breathe the "oxygen" of Heaven which is the essence of the Glory. Thus when they manifest in this earthly realm, they come bringing the breath of heaven, the Glory.

Likewise when we find that Secret Place of the Most High and learn to abide in His Divine Presence, we will also breathe the "oxygen" or atmosphere of the Glory. It will permeate our being and we will become "atmosphere changers", bringing the atmosphere of Heaven wherever we go. The atmosphere of Heaven's Glory is an atmosphere of harmony, peace, and pure love. It is a deep awareness that God has passed by and touched our lives.

Every person carries an "atmosphere" that goes beyond the words they speak. Some people call them the "vibes" others give off. It is said that communication is only 30% verbal and 70% non verbal.[5] You may not always remember all of the words that someone speaks, but you will always remember how you felt when you were around them.

If someone has been in a room full of cigarette smoke, you can tell where they have been. Even if they themselves have not been smoking, they carry the "atmosphere" of cigarette smoke. If someone has been involved in unclean activities they will carry an "unclean atmosphere" If someone is bitter or angry, they will carry that atmosphere. If one is bowed down with cares, fear, doubt or anxiety, they will also bring this kind of an atmosphere.

When we come into the presence of others, what "atmosphere" do we leave behind? Is there a fragrance of having been with Jesus? Do we have the ability to bring peace in the midst of strife and chaos? Can we bring healing balm for the wounded soul? Does one sense the Love of God flowing to them from us? These precious virtues can only be found in the Secret Place of His Holy Presence.

Where there was once strife, contention and jealousy, the Love of God will be shed abroad in our hearts. No evil, unclean force can remain in the presence of true Glory. Glory will cleanse, deliver and heal. If anything presumes to remain in the presence of Glory it will be judged. It is a consuming fire. *"Our God is a consuming fire"* **Hebrews 12:29**

A true encounter with Glory will sanctify us. It will permeate our being, and the brilliance of it will emanate from our countenance. I have seen, when the Glory of God comes on a countenance, it lifts the countenance and rejuvenates the person. It even takes away the appearance of any wrinkles and makes one look years younger! The Glory brings a supernatural enabling that is beyond human limitations.

We must learn how to walk with the Lord in such a way that we can carry His atmosphere wherever we go. This happens by spending time with Him, loving Him, learning to honor and reverence His Holy Presence. We must always be careful to not grieve the Holy Spirit, that He not distance Himself nor depart from us. If we do grieve Him or another of His children, we must immediately repent and seek to draw close once again. It is learning to "practice His Presence". We must love and reverence His Presence, before He will lead us into the secret treasures of His Glory.

This is another dimension altogether. It is not bringing our prayer petitions, singing songs to the Lord, spiritual warfare prayers, or even praying in the Spirit. One can pray hours a day and yet never connect with the heart of the Father in intimate communion. It is not about the motion or dynamics of prayer. It is about love and passion for Him.

This is about an abiding love relationship and communion. Whether we speak, or are silent. Whether, we worship, or we weep. It is learning to cultivate and abide in the Lord's Holy Presence and learning to be sensitive to His Holy Spirit.

God is restoring to us the elements that bring His Glory, and when the conditions are right, He will come in His Glory.

Glory comes from the realm of eternity and timelessness. Therefore the Glory is not bound by natural laws of gravity, time or distance. When we are in the Glory we are under a supernatural influence.

Glory in the Nations

There have been several outstanding times, over the years, as I have ministered in the nations of the world, that God has come in Glory encounters. Each of these encounters has been marked by the same characteristics of God's Glory. In each instance there is a supernatural weightiness of His manifest presence, in a white, misty or bright cloud in the atmosphere. There have been times when even tongues of fire have manifest. These times have usually been accompanied by some kind of sign, wonder, healing, deliverance or repentance.

Fireball in Ushuaia: (in Argentina, the southernmost city of the world) Several years ago on a particular afternoon, the leadership of the church where I was ministering had arranged a special women's gathering, open to all Christian women in the city. After the message, the women were gathered at the altar, seeking the Lord, and awaiting special ministry. I also, had paused a moment in prayer, before continuing to minister.

At that moment, there was an extremely bright light that "exploded" like a fireball in the room. It was the intensity of one of those, huge, old fashion flashes used to take portrait pictures back in the 1800's. For a few seconds it was blinding, but no one had a camera or a flash. Everyone had their eyes closed in prayer. There were gasps among the people and we could feel a heavy weight of God's Glory descend. It seemed that everything went into slow motion. Women began to collapse to the ground with no one touching them. It was a powerful encounter, and only lasted a few moments, but, I believe that the fruit was eternal.

The Glory Knows No Borders: Recently, I had the privilege of ministering in a predominantly Muslim nation. We were in a radical Muslim area, where in recent years, many churches had been burned and many Christians massacred. These Christians serve and have been faithful to the Lord, at a great price and under much persecution. Many have suffered the loss of family, friends and their church buildings, where they congregated. The "Church" had in a sense gone "underground". Some pastors were very discouraged and were losing the fire of the vision that once burned bright within them.

In one particular service, we saw the visitation of God's Glory. As the pastor and the congregation were at the altar in prayer, the fire of God was so intense in the room that one could literally sense the tongues of fire over the people's heads, as they wept and cried out to the Lord. Many were being healed from the trauma and pain of their great losses and persecution and being filled afresh with the fire of God.

The pastor testified of his personal visitation from the Lord. He said that he was "caught away" to another place and was totally unaware of his natural surroundings. He said the Lord was personally ministering to him, talking to him, touching him, and healing him inside. He could feel the Lord pouring fresh fire into him. He testified that it was as strong as an encounter as the night that he was first called into the ministry, many years ago.

Heavenly Portals

The Greek word for "portal" is (thura) or door. It says a portal provides an opening or closure, both literally or figuratively. It is a doorway that connects two distant locations separated by time or space. It can be a grand or imposing entrance as in "the portals of heaven" that connects the natural and spiritual realm.

Heavenly Portals from God, come from the third heaven as mentioned in:

2 Corinthians 12:2 *"I knew a man in Christ above fourteen years ago, (whether in the body I cannot tell; or whether out of the body I cannot tell: God knoweth) such an one caught up to the third heaven." These portals are for presence, communication, protection, provision worship, transportation and angelic ministry.*

We will mention nine kinds of portals that will be open for God's people in these end-times. Glory Portals, Personal Portals, Regional Portals, House of Worship Portals, Angelic Portals, Time Portals, Prophetic Portals, Seasonal Portals and Ancient Portals. We are seeing an increase of supernatural activity and divine intervention from God in this way.

Glory Portals: All heavenly portals, in actuality are Glory Portals that are for the manifestation of God's glory in one form or another. All testify of the Glory of the Lord. There are times when the Glory of the Lord will "suddenly" appear in His Temple, to His beloved who delight in Him.

"Behold, I will send my messenger, and he shall prepare the way before me; and the Lord, whom ye seek, shall suddenly come to His temple. . . .but who may abide the day of His coming? And who shall stand when He appeareth? For He is like refiner's fire and like fuller's soap." **Malachi 1:1-2**

There are also times when the manifest Glory of the Lord accompanied by the Fear of the Lord may suddenly appear before the unbeliever or mocker as a witness. When these Glory Portals have a visible manifestation they may appear as round cylinders or shafts of thick, brilliant white or golden light. Angels, or the Lord Himself may appear in this instance. This is becoming a frequent and common manifestation in the Muslim world where the Glory of the Lord is manifest and Jesus Himself appears. Many Muslims are coming to Christ because of these kinds of supernatural Glory encounters.

Manifest Presence of Jesus: As we arrived at the church, in Buenos Aires, Argentina that morning, it seemed that it would be a regular Sunday morning worship service, but the Lord had a wonderful surprise for us! At one point in worship, there was a spontaneous touch of Glory that took us into another dimension. When the worship finished, as I came to the pulpit, I felt the fear of the Lord, that I dare not say or do anything to break the Holiness of that moment.

One thing that I have always learned is that to be able to carry the anointing and host the move of the Holy Spirit in a service, what you have to say or contribute must be the same level of anointing, or higher than what just happened previously. Otherwise it is best to just be quiet.

At that moment, as I opened my Bible, and looked out over the congregation, I had an open vision of Jesus walking into the sanctuary. He was dressed in a purple robe. His eyes were like fire and very intent. It was clear that He was there on a mission. I paused as I was unsure what to do with what I was seeing. Should I hold it? Should I speak it out? With much fear and trembling I spoke it out. At that moment there was an incredible shift in the atmosphere, as the manifest Presence of Jesus filled the room. Some people fell to their knees sobbing and weeping, others continued to worship and others sat still, as if they were frozen in time.

For one hour and a half I was afraid to move, as Jesus Himself moved through the congregation, ministering to the people. For one week afterward, testimonies came in of healings from cancer, diabetes, insomnia etc. Others were delivered from depression, mental disorders and addictions. Others received guidance for major decisions. Some responded to the call of God, and stepped into new places of ministry. Some had financial breakthroughs. No one had to bring a prayer request. No healing line was formed. No one laid hands on anyone. Jesus laid His Hand on everyone, and virtue flowed out! When Jesus is in the house all is well!

Personal Portals: God has His conditions that draw His Glory to us and cause the heavens to open over us. This was true in the Old Testament and it remains true today. If we will align with God's conditions and walk in a way that is pleasing to Him, He will be faithful to meet us and pour out a blessing that we cannot contain.

Enoch was a man who walked with God, in evil and corrupt times, but it was said of Enoch that he had this testimony, that he pleased God.

Hebrews 11:5 *"By faith Enoch was translated that he should not see death; and was not found, because God had translated him; for before his translation he had this testimony, that he pleased God."*

Enoch walked close with God and there was a heavenly portal open to him. He just crossed the threshold into the other side from time into eternity. As we mentioned, the Glory is not bound by gravity, time or distance. Enoch walked in the Glory. He walked in such a way that caused a personal portal to be open over his life.

Some of God's conditions that will draw the Glory to us are:

1. **Holiness**: *"follow peace with all men, and holiness, without which no man shall see the Lord"* **Hebrews 12:14**

2. **Purity**: *"Who shall ascend into the hill of the Lord" or who shall stand in His Holy Place? He that hath clean hands and a pure heart; who hath not lifted up his soul unto vanity, nor sworn deceitfully."* **Psalms 24:3-4**

3. **The Fear of the Lord**: *"Behold, the eye of the Lord is upon them that fear Him, upon them that hope in His mercy, to deliver their soul from death and to keep them alive in famine.* **Psalm 33:18-19**

4. **Prayer**: *"And the smoke of the incense, which came with the prayers of the saints, ascended*

up before God out of the angel's hand."
Revelations 8:4

5. **Fasting:** *"Therefore also now, saith the Lord,
   turn ye even to me with all of your heart,
   and with fasting, and with weeping, and with
   mourning,"* **Joel 2:12**

6. **Unity**: *"And when the day of Pentecost was
   fully come, they were all with one accord in
   one place. And suddenly there came a sound
   from heaven as of a rushing mighty wind, and
   it filled al the house where they were sitting.
   And there appeared unto them cloven tongues
   like as of fire, and it sat upon each of them."*
   Acts 2:1-3

7. **Worship:** *"It came to pass, as the trumpeters
   and singers were as one, to make one sound
   to be heard in praising, and thanking the
   Lord; and when they lifted up their voice with
   the trumpets and instruments of musick, and
   praised the Lord, saying for He is good, His
   mercy endureth for ever: that then the house
   was filled with a cloud, even the house of
   the Lord; so that the priests could not stand
   to minister by reason of the cloud, even the
   house of the Lord."* **2 Chronicles 5:13-14**

8. **Brokenness:** *"The Lord is nigh unto them that are of a broken heart; and saveth such that be of a contrite spirit."* **Psalm 34:18**

As we mentioned before, especially as the days get darker, it is vital that we contend for our faith, press into the secret place, and believe God to open up His heavenly portals over our lives, our homes, our churches and our regions.

"Arise, shine; for thy light is come, and the Glory of the Lord is risen upon thee. For behold the darkness shall cover the earth and gross darkness the people; but the Lord shall arise upon thee." **Isaiah 60: 1**

"House of Worship Portals": In these end-times we are going to see God strategically placing His "Houses of Worship" all over the face of the earth. These will be places where the Glory of God has come and resides. There will be open portals over these places. They will be houses of healing where supernatural moves of the Holy Spirit will be common place. Some will be large congregations. Others will be house churches. Some will be groups of believers, meeting in the marketplace, while others will be secret believers meeting, in hidden places. There will be a common denominator among all of them. They will be those who have paid the price to meet God's conditions for Glory. They will be those who have set their house in order to draw the Glory of God to them.

That is how it was at the dedication of the Temple by King Solomon. The temple had been built, prepared and set in order according to God's pattern and conditions. After the Ark had been brought in and the priesthood sanctified, Solomon lifted his voice to the Lord and he earnestly prayed for God's perpetual Covenant and Glory to abide with them. **(2 Chronicles 6-7)**

It says in **2 Chronicles 7:1** *"Now when Solomon had made an end of praying, the fire came down from heaven, and consumed the burnt offering and the sacrifices; and the Glory of the Lord filled the house."*

But that was not all! Further on in the chapter, it says that the Lord appeared unto Solomon by night and said that his prayer had been heard. The Lord said that he had chosen that place for Himself, as a "House of Sacrifice"

So what does it mean to be a "House of Sacrifice"? It means that God's conditions were met. It means that Solomon found favor in the sight of the Lord, and God established His abiding covenant with them. It means that even if there is famine, draught or plague in the land, that when the voices of God's people are raised in prayer from that "House of Sacrifice", that God will hear their prayer and heal the land. And if by chance, God's hand of judgment

60

be averted! It means, that His eyes are upon that place and that His heart is there perpetually.

2 Chronicles 7:12-16 *"And the Lord appeared to Solomon by night, and said unto him, I have heard thy prayer, and have chosen this place to myself for an house of sacrifice. If I shut up heaven that there be no rain, or if I command the locust to devour the land, or if I send pestilence among my people; if my people who are called by my name shall humble themselves, and pray, and seek my face, and turn from their wicked ways; then will I hear from heaven, and will forgive their sin, and will heal their land. Now mine eyes shall be open, and mine ears attent unto the prayer that is made in this place. For now have I chosen and sanctified this house, that my name may be there for ever: and mine eyes and mine heart shall be there perpetually."*

Oh, how we need for God to raise up "Houses of Sacrifice" in this hour where His heart and His Glory abide; that God may truly have a covenant people who will rule and reign with Christ Jesus in heavenly places with true, Godly power and authority! That the forces of hell that seek to devour, shall be pushed back, and the hand of God's judgment be stayed in this hour.

Regional Portals: Another kind of portal that we will see more evident is the regional portal. When natural disasters increase and we see unprecedented destruction on every hand and recession and unemployment abound. We will see God begin to open these portals over the property and regions of the righteous. Just as He established the land of Goshen in the midst of famine stricken Egypt for the children of Israel, so shall He mark and protect the land and property of the righteous.

Goshen was a fertile, rich land with plenty of water for crops and plenty of green pastureland for livestock to graze. Goshen was in the same region and within the same boarders of Egypt, but, yet, Egypt was in draught and famine. How could this be, that there was such a different climate and protection over that area? A regional portal of God's blessing and protection was open over them because they were a covenant people. Even when the plagues began and Pharoah would not let the Children of Israel depart, Goshen's boarders were marked and the plagues could not touch the land of Goshen.

Exodus 8:22-23 *"And I will sever in that day the land of Goshen, in which my people dwell, that no swarms of flies shall be there; to the end that thou mayest know that I am the Lord in the midst of the earth. And I will put a division between my people and thy people: tomorrow shall this sign be."*

Last summer I was reading a news article on the internet about how the recession had hit so many parts of the country. The article mentioned a place called

Goshen County, Wyoming that had not been affected by the recession. I had to smile. It was as if God was giving a prophetic sign of what was to come.

Along with walking with God in a way that pleases Him, there seems to be a direct link with the protection of our land and possessions and tithing and giving to God, that opens this kind of regional portal. Giving sets spiritual laws of provision and protection in motion.

It says in **Malachi 3:10-11** *"Bring ye all the tithes into the storehouse, that there may be meat in mine house, and prove me now herewith, saith the Lord of Hosts, if I will not open you the windows of heaven, and pour you out a blessing, that there shall not be room enough to receive it. And I will rebuke the devourer for your sakes, and he shall not destroy the fruits of your ground; neither shall your vine cast her fruit before the time in the field, saith the Lord of Hosts."*

We have all heard testimonies over the years of farmers who's crops have been spared from sudden hail storms and how peoples homes have been protected from fires and tornadoes.

There have been two specific times in my life that I remember watching with my own eyes, God supernaturally protect property.

Fire: One of these occasions was when a team of us were doing mission work at a retreat center in Honduras. There was a forest fire burning in the area. One afternoon as I was teaching on intercession, a lady ran into the building, frantically warning that the forest fire was burning right up against the property on three sides. The only access road out was closed off because of the raging fire. We were definitely in a desperate situation, and needed God's Divine intervention. We decided it was time to put into practice what we had learned. We all spontaneously got up and marched out to the edge of the property, facing the raging flames. We proclaimed a line of the Blood of Jesus to surround the property and began to pray that the fire would be quenched. As we spoke out for God's protection, instantly, at that moment, a strong wind came up and turned the fire back in a completely different direction. We saw how the fire had taken acre after acre of forest land. It was swift enough that it could have destroyed the entire camp. The fire had come right up to the property line but did not cross over. It was very clear that God had set a very detailed mark of protection around the property line.

Tornado: The second time was here at our International Headquarter property. It was during tornado season. A warning came, that a tornado had been sighted in the nearby area. We all ran and took cover in a special room in the administration building. We could hear the tornado get closer and closer. It sounded like a freight train passing over us. When the "all clear" signal was given, we stepped outside. To our amazement the entire back side of a neighboring restaurant had been ripped off and blown apart. The tornado had made a clear path of destruction down the side of the mountain till it got directly at our property line, right behind some of the buildings. But right there the tornado lifted it's tail and went over the top of us, touching down again 2 miles on the other side. Nothing on the property was touched or destroyed.

God has made provision for His own. He wants us to have the assurance in our hearts that He will supernaturally protect us and intervene for us in these days.

In Regional Portals we can also see areas of revival, where God is soveriegnly moving in one area and not another. The Argentina revival is an incredible example of God's eyes being upon an entire region or nation.

The Great Argentina Revival: Although, one could fill volumes telling of the incredible events and encounters of this great revival, I want to just share a short account of what I experienced first hand.

It was back in the 1980's, when I was 22 years old, and just beginning in the ministry. This was a sovereign time of visitation over the entire nation of Argentina. God raised up and was using mightily, a man by the name of Carlos Annacondia, as an evangelist, in mass crusades. Literally millions of souls came to the Lord during that time period.

The crusades were marked by mass healing and deliverance. There were accounts of people being slain in the Spirit in public buses, as they passed by the crusade sight.

There was a man in Buenos Aires who owned a bar on a side street, where one of the crusades was being held. Night after night, as multitudes gathered for the crusade, his business remained empty. On night he stepped out of the bar and raised his fist to God, in anger. He was struck down as dead, by the Power of God! The EMT's came and were loading him onto the ambulance, when he finally "came to". When he became conscience, he told of how he had been visited by Jesus. He gave his heart to the Lord, and within the week, his entire family was saved and serving the Lord!

During this time, hundreds of new churches were established and others grew to multi-thousand member congregations. Various church groups took over dozens of the cities opera theaters and cultural centers, turning them into churches.

One of these converted theaters that I have ministered in, could only seat 5,000 people at a time. It was open and operating as a church seven days a week, from 6:00 am in the morning till 12 midnight every night. People would stand in line for two blocks long, waiting in the heat, cold, rain and shine, to get into service. Each member had a set time when they were allocated to attend their service. Many times the pastors would have to announce, "If you have been in service once today, please leave, so that the next group can get in". The hunger for God was great.

We would see drug addicts come in off the street and be gloriously saved and delivered. They hadn't even heard a message, a song or an altar call! The atmosphere of conviction and Glory was in the streets! This truly is what you would call a "Heavenly Portal" over an entire region.

Angelic Portals: There are established Angelic Portals where Ministering Angels ascend and descend from heaven to earth. This is their point of access between eternity and time.

Genesis 28:12 *"And he dreamed, and behold a ladder set up on the earth, and the top of it reached to heaven: and behold the angels of God ascending and descending on it."*

There are many ranks and types of Angels that carry out their special duties upon the earth and on our behalf.

There are special Ministering Angels that come and tend to God's people in times of suffering, special need or danger. The Greek word for minister means to serve or assist. These angels come with the compassionate Love of God to minister peace, comfort and healing in time of suffering.[6] They come to silently stand guard in time of danger. I'm sure we will never know, this side of Heaven, the countless times that our Ministering Angels have protected us from evil, danger and even death. There are times in special encounters, that God supernaturally lifts the veil and allows the angels to be visible to our natural eyes.

There are times when these angels come to give special guidance when we don't know what to do or where to turn. It can be either for spiritual guidance or when we are lost geographically, and need help to find the right way.

Exodus 23:20 *"Behold, I send an Angel before thee, to keep thee in the way, and to bring thee into the place which I have prepared"*

We have heard of "Angels on Assignment". Well, I believe that Angels assist us when we are on assignment and we need special guidance to get to our assignment.

Well, this time I didn't know that I was on assignment, but God did! I remember one time when I was just a young Christian. I had a photography job and I was driving back home to spend the weekend with my parents in South Dakota.

As I was driving through a town in Nebraska that I had never been to before, I felt a very clear prompting that said: "turn left and park in the parking lot of this hospital." When I parked, I heard "enter the hospital and go to the 5th floor waiting room". I had no idea that it would be the intensive care unit waiting room. There were just two people in this intensive care unit. As I entered the waiting room, a young man looked up at me and said: "Oh, you must be here for the other family". I said: "actually God sent me". The man looked at me with a stunned look, lifted his newspaper in front of him and said: "yea, right!" He then took his turn and went to see his family member, as the other family came back into the waiting room. They also looked at me and said: "oh, you must be here for the other family." I again said: "no, actually God sent me." The woman broke down and began to weep. She said: "I have been praying that God would send someone to pray for us and to pray for our daughter!" They were from out of town and had had a terrible accident where someone had run over their 9 year old daughter. She was in a coma in critical condition. They knew absolutely no one in that area. I know there were Ministering Angels that day assisting me and tending to them in their suffering and grief.

I could tell of other occasions where God had clearly sent His angels to minister, guide and assist. But, maybe that will be for another time or another book.

Messenger Angels: There are also Messenger Angels that come to earth with special messages at special times. Usually these are the Archangels. An example of this was when Gabriel appeared to Mary, announcing that she was highly favored of

God and that she was chosen to give birth to the Savior, Jesus.

Luke 1:26-33 (vs 28) *"And the angel came in unto her, and said, Hail, thou art highly favored, the Lord is with thee: blessed art thou among women."*

Angels in Worship: All angels are created to be Worship Angels. They are very sensitive to our worship here. There are times when the angels join in with our worship to the Lord. Sometimes on these occasions one can feel that the room is filled with angels. There may come a special enhancement that seems to assist our worship in it's ascent to the Father. There are other times in worship where you get the feeling that the angels decided to "sit that one out" or to step aside while we do "our thing". Sometimes our worship even saddens and grieves them.

There was one specific time, in a special revival service, when the worship ascended to a very high realm and we could hear what seemed to be a multiplication of voices far beyond the number of people in the service. There came a "holy hush" that settled upon the people. As everyone got silent, you could audibly hear the voices of the Angel Choir continue to sing. This was a breathtaking, incredible experience.

I also know of another instance when, a small group were gathered together for worship practice. They audibly heard the angels join in the worship and were actually able to capture it on tape! I

70

personally know of these people and have listened to this tape.

Even though demonic activity is increasing in these days, God's supernatural activity and ministry of angels is also increasing. God is opening up His portals and giving His people many more glimpses behind the veil between the natural and the supernatural realms.

Instruments Prophecy in Worship: This particular meeting was the last service of a special, 3 day conference, in the city of Mendoza, Argentina. People came from several provinces in the area to attend the conference.

There was a very special atmosphere of the Presence of the Lord throughout the conference. The people had prepared with prayer and fasting beforehand for this event. They were hungry to see God move in their midst.

The message ended on a very high note. There was much joy and rejoicing in the air. The worship team was standing ready for the altar call. Well there was none. As the orchestra began to play, I noticed that the Spirit of the Lord was upon them in a very powerful way with the most incredible crescendos I have ever heard this side of Heaven. I stepped forward and began to "conduct" the orchestra. Well, naturally speaking this is something I know nothing about. I would watch the Spirit of the Lord move on one instrument after another, as I called upon them to play. Each one was prophesying in turn under the direction of the Holy Spirit! The Lord was getting for Himself some worship, Heaven's style and the Angels were joining, in their full strength! As this continued the tangible weighty Glory cloud filled the sanctuary. Healings and deliverances sponta- neously began to occur throughout the congrega- tion. The Glory was notably there and the people responded and reached directly into the Glory for their needs. The Lord met them in a wonderful way!

Prophetic Portals: Although the gift of prophecy is quit common these days. God is restoring and opening up the realm of the prophetic more and more in this season.

There is a high realm of the prophetic that we are increasingly seeing. These are prophetic portals where God supernaturally opens a door into heaven and calls His prophets to "come up hither" This was true for Daniel and many other old testament prophets. They were called of God to leave a detailed record of things to come. Many were required to prophecy of things that were not yet known to man or never had been seen before. They needed a vivid encounter that enveloped all of their senses so that they could accurately record in "virtual reality" what they were seeing and experiencing. These were accurate, detailed words that would form and mark history and be bridges between dispensations.

God is once again opening these prophetic por- tals for His end-time prophets as we cross over into another new dispensation.

John on the Isle of Patmos was also caught up into the third heaven and the End-Time Revelation was unfolded before him.

Revelation 4:1 says: *"After this I looked, and behold a door was open in heaven: and the first voice which I heard was as it were a trumpet talking with me; which said, Come up hither, and I will shew you things that must be hereafter."*

There are modern day prophets living today that continue to have these kind of encounters and I believe they will increase as we enter more into the End-Times.

Time Portals: We spoke earlier of Enoch and how he walked with God and was not, because God translated him. He stepped across the threshold of the portal between time and eternity.

Philip was another example of someone stepping through the time portal God opened up to him after he had ministered to the Ethiopian Eunuch. Wow! Talk about a "sudden" change of plans! Philip was baptizing the Eunuch and before he could even come up out of the water, he was caught away by the Spirit of the Lord and found himself in the city of Azotus, beginning a whole new preaching itin-erary. This was a time portal that opened for Philip, transporting him from one geographical location to another, bypassing time and distance.

Acts 8:38-40: *"And he commanded the chariot to stand still: and they went down both into the water, both Philip and the eunuch; and he baptized him. And when they were come up out of the water, the Spirit of the Lord caught away Philip, that the eunuch saw him no more: and he went on his way rejoicing. But Philip was found at Azotus: and passing through, he preached in all the cities, till he came to Caesarea."*

We have heard of testimonies of this happening to pastors and believers in persecuted lands in the face of imminent danger. The Spirit of the Lord, comes and catches them away to another place where they are safe and they continue to preach the Gospel. We will hear of this happening more and more in the lives of believers as the times require.

Gwen Shaw tells of an illiterate woman during an outpouring of the Holy Spirit in Taiwan, who was "caught away" for hours in the presence of the Lord. She was taken back to experience detailed events during Bible Times. The beautiful thing was, you knew it was genuine, because the woman had no prior knowledge of the Bible. Yet, she shared in detail these encounters, which aligned perfectly with the Word of God. This is another example of a time portal. This woman was transported back in time.

Transported by His Glory: Many years ago in the summer of 1982, I had a very real and powerful encounter in the Glory. When I awoke that summer morning I remember it was sunny and the birds were singing. I went to my regular place of prayer in the living room and began to pray. That morning I had a very strong, unusual feeling. It was as if there was a burning fireball on the inside of me. As I continued to pray in the Holy Spirit that fireball began to come up out of me. As it was coming out my mouth, I found myself standing in Red Square in Russia. In the body or out I do not know. But I could literally feel the cobblestone under my feet. It was a cloudy and drizzling day, the air was cool and damp. As I stood positioned I began to prophecy that Communism come down and the Jews would be released to return to Israel. At that time, I was a young Christian and in the natural, really knew nothing about the issue of the Jews returning to Israel from Russia. The incredible thing about this encounter was that when I returned to the living room, I was standing in the exact stance as I was when the encounter began, but it was three hours later. Ten years later to the month, the Lord gave me the privilege of going to Red Square. When I arrived, I was able to identify and go to the **exact** spot and position that I had stood giving this prophecy ten years before! Yes, by that time Communism in Russia had come down and the Jews had been released to return to Israel. I had stepped into a place of timelessness that was not bound by gravity, time nor distance in the Glory. It was a Heavenly Portal that had opened, connecting Heaven and earth.

Seasonal Portals: These portals are connected with the Feasts of Israel. There are certain times of year, when believers, as they have followed this Biblical pattern and observed the Feasts of the Lord have experienced greater manifestation of God's Glory in their meetings.[7]

Also, those who observe a Sabbath day of rest will find special, deeper rest and presence of the Lord during that time.

God honors and blesses those who honor and bless Israel. In **Genesis 12:3** the Lord says of Israel: *"I will bless them that bless thee, and curse him that curseth thee"*.

This will be a great test for believers in this hour, as the whole world seems to be taking a stand against Israel. But when you stand for Israel and bless her, you shall surely see the Hand of God's blessing and favor come upon your life.

Seasonal portals can also be correlated with seasons when God is speaking a specific emphasis or prophetic word. When we respond in obedience to what God is saying, there is a special grace at that season for change, healing, deliverance or breakthrough. In what would normally take years and maybe many tears to step into the fullness of the work that God can do in just a few moments of time in our lives.

Honduras Visitation: For several years we (End-Time Handmaidens) would hold an International School of Ministry in Tegucigalpa, Honduras.

Pastors and leaders would come from all over Honduras, Nicaragua and El Salvador to be a part of this school. It was always a very rich time in the Word of God and in the Presence of the Lord. But this particular school had a special mark of Glory on it, from the first day.

There was a man from the remote jungles of Honduras on the eastern (Mesquita) coast, who worked as a professional diver for lobster. He was injured in a diving accident, two years prior, that left him paralyzed from the waist down. In his remote village he didn't have access to crutches or wheel-chairs or anything to aid him with his disability. He got around by "walking" with his arms and drag-ging his body behind him.

When word came to his village that we were coming to Honduras; he felt the Lord wanted him to be in the school. Well, it was a five hour journey just to get down river by boat, then, he must take a twelve hour bus ride to get to Tegucigalpa. It was a daunting prospect, to even consider, how the Lord would make a way for him to come. But he was determined and he set his face as flint. Nothing was going to stand in his way! He began his journey in this manner and the Lord sent "angels" to help him along the way. By the grace and help of God, he arrived, and was there for the entire school.

The very first night during worship, the Lord healed him by His own hand! Just as the man in the book of Acts, he stood to his feet, walking and leaping and praising God!

Acts 3:7-8 *"And he (Peter) took him by the right hand, and lifted him up: and immediately his feet and ankle bones received strength. And he leaping up stood, and walked and entered with them into the temple, walking and leaping and praising God."*

When the people saw him leaping and dancing before the Lord, it released an explosion of God's Glory that continued in a sovereign visitation throughout the entire school.

This man had sought for healing and had not found it where he was, so he pressed through, to a place where there was a portal of healing open for him.

"Caught Up" in a Trance: Also, in this same school, one fifteen year old young man was caught up in a trance for three hours. During this encounter, he had a visitation from Jesus, who told him He was placing the gift of healing in his hands. So, when he "came to" and he shared his experience, we immediately had him begin to pray for the people. There was a great flow of healing released that night.

A trance is a biblical term for an "open vision" except lasting for longer periods of time than a normal vision. The Greek word for trance is "ekstasis" meaning amazement, astonishment, to take one out of their natural state of thought. It can be found mentioned in:

Acts 10:9-11 (*vs 10b-11a*) *"but while they made ready, he fell into a trance, and saw heaven opened . . ."*

Acts 11:5a *"I was in the city of Joppa praying: and in a trance I saw a vision"*

Acts 22:17-18 *"And it came to pass, that, when I was come again to Jerusalem, even while I prayed in the temple, I was in a trance; and saw Him saying unto me, Make haste and get thee quickly out of Jerusalem: for they will not receive the testimony concerning me.*

Trances were a marked and common sign in Evangelist, Maria Woodworth Etter's ministry during the period between 1880 and 1924. She was dubbed the "trance evangelist". In one service alone, it is recorded that fifteen souls came running and screaming to the altar for mercy and were caught up into trances. She was considered among the Vanguard leaders of the Pentecostal movement

Ancient Portals: These portals or gates have their origins in ancient times. Some of these gates have been barred, over nations, for centuries because of ruling principalities and powers over these nations. This has hindered the Gospel and the moving of the Holy Spirit in these places. But God is opening the ancient gates and the great light of Jesus Christ shall shine in these closed nations, tribes and people groups. God is going to reveal His hidden riches in secret places. I believe this is speaking of spiritual revelation but it also refers to souls "hidden" or lost in great darkness that shall be released by the Power of God in this great End-Time Harvest that is just before us. Every tribe, tongue and nation shall declare that Jesus Christ is Lord!

Isaiah 45: 1-3 *prophetically declares this: "Thus saith the Lord to Cyrus, whose right hand I have holden, to subdue nations before him; and I will loose the loins of kings, to open before him the two-leaved gates; and the gates shall not be shut; I will go before thee, and make the crooked places straight: I will break in pieces the gates of brass, and cut in sunder the bars of iron: And I will give thee the treasures of darkness, and hidden riches of secret places, that thou mayest know that I, the Lord, which call thee by thy name, am the God of Israel."*

Second heaven portals: I do want to just briefly comment that the term "portal" is used by the "New Age" people. But their "connection" is from the second heaven. The second heaven is where the principalities and powers and rulers of the darkness dwell as mentioned in **Ephesians 6:12** *"For we wrestle not against flesh and blood but against principalities, against powers, against the rulers of the darkness of this world, against spiritual wickedness in high places."* Another scripture that talks of second heaven interference is **Daniel 10:12-13**

"Then said he unto me, fear not, Daniel for from the first day that thou didst set thine heart to understand, and to chasten thyself before thy God, thy words were heard, and I am come for thy words. But the prince of the kingdom of Persia withstood me one and twenty days; but, lo, Micheal, one of the chief princes, came to help me; . . ."

We need not be fearful about using this term. It began with God. The "new Age" also use the symbol of the rainbow, but God created the rainbow.

The Coming Storm

For many years we as American's have lived in a "blessed" nation. But we are living in times when the darkness is closing in quickly. Not only America but multitudes and nations are taking things into their own hands. God's blessing and protection are lifting and great storms are on the horizon.

This is why it is vital that we listen to the voice of the prophets to "come up higher" and prepare ourselves a Holy Habitation to weather the storm. God has a place of divine protection and defense for the righteous, for His Bride.

Isaiah 40:31 *"But they that wait upon the Lord shall renew their strength, they shall mount up with wings as eagles; they shall run, and not be weary, they shall walk, and not faint".*

"Did you know that an eagle knows when a storm is approaching long before the storm breaks? The eagle will fly to a high place and wait for the winds to come. When the storm hits, it sets it's wings so that the wind will pick it up and lift it above the storm. While the storm rages below, the eagle is soaring above it. The eagle does not escape the storm. It simply uses the storm to lift it higher. The eagle rises on the very winds that bring the storm."⁸ This is how we can learn to survive and even thrive in the midst of the storm.

Isaiah 26:20 *says: "Come, my people, enter thou into thy chambers, and shut thy doors about thee: hide thyself as it were for a little moment, until the indignation be over past.*

The word "Chambers" here in the Hebrew is the same root as is used in **Psalm 91: 1** for "Secret Place.

When it says: "hide thyself as it were" does not mean that we flee to a physical hidden place and shut ourselves off in fear of what is to come. There are some believers that are doing just that. They are making great provisions for the flesh with food and armaments to hide away from the storms and crisis. However, they do not have the peace or security of the Lord in their hearts or the touch of Glory upon their lives. I would rather prepare in the Glory and let Him lead me under the canopy of His divine protection and provision.

I do want to clarify, though, that it is wise to have some form of supplies and provision laid up for a season, but this must not be our major focus.

We must rise like the eagle with the winds of the Spirit. If we will listen and get quiet before the Lord we will find that the winds are approaching, the winds that will lift us to a higher place. God will teach us how to fly by the radar of His Spirit and not by our natural understanding. We will find that the laws of the Spirit will work for us! These laws are totally opposite to the natural laws of the "spirit of this age". When we are in the flesh, earthly, natural laws apply. In the Glory, heavens laws apply. Live by the law of love, holiness, forgiveness and giving. There will be many strong forces unleashed from hell that will try to cause us to live just the opposite. But keep these virtues by the strength and grace of God and the laws of the Spirit will operate in your life.

Remember that in every major storm there is always an "eye of the storm" which is a region of mostly calm weather, found at the center of the storm. The "eye of the storm" is surrounded by the storm wall which is the ring or area where the strongest, most severe weather occurs. But in the "eye of the storm" it is characterized by light breezes and clear skies.[9]

This is a very good analogy of a "heavenly portal" A clearing or open door between heaven and earth that makes way for God's blessing and provision in the midst of the darkest, most raging storms.

Psalm 91:7-9 *"A thousand shall fall at thy side and ten thousand at thy right hand; but it shall not come nigh thee. Only with thine eyes shalt thou behold the reward of the wicked, because thou hast made the Lord, even the most High, thy habitation."*

Practical Preparations

As well as the Spiritual preparation there are some practical things that we can do to prepare for and survive the storm.

1. Do not be afraid or immediately assume the worst because of the fear tactics of media hype. Get quiet and listen to God. Fear is a powerful motivator to rule the multitudes in these end-times, but, Love is a more powerful motivator.

2. Get out of debt. Simplify your lifestyle. Do not live beyond your means. It is wise to make practical provisions for anticipated needs. In case of emergency it is good to have at least 30 days supply of food, water, fuel for heating and for automobiles and money set aside.

3. Do not stop giving! This is what will keep the supernatural law of provision working for you, even in the midst of great economical crisis. "If what you have is not enough for your need, make it your seed!"

4. Stay focused, on the Lord and not on the problems. Keep your standard high. Live by godly principles, not by the pressure of the circumstances.

5. Stay close to, and reconnect with **trusted** friends and family. There is strength in numbers of those who are tried and proven. Those who are significant in your life, whom will love you and pray for you. Walk with those who walk in the unity of the Spirit. There is power in prayer and unity, especially in times of treachery and betrayal.[10]

Covenant Relationships

There is a great importance in establishing "covenant relationships" in these end-times. We must be in covenant relationship with the Lord and with one another.

In general, the Body of Christ, as it stands today is too loosely knit one to another. We will love one another if does not cost or inconvenience us or until an "offense" comes along. We see so few, true, trusted, covenant relationships in the church today with those whom we are closely knit in the Spirit by love and trust. How many people do we really have in our lives that we truly feel we can trust our heart to, and trust our name on their lips in times of struggle? Those that will pull away and criticize us today, or scrutinize our actions in suspicion, before they will pray for us, and believe the best of us, are those who will, under pressure, betray us tomorrow. We must also examine our own heart and love walk. Can the Lord trust others hearts and lives into our care?

"But if we walk in the light as He is in the light, we have fellowship one with another and the Blood of Jesus Christ His son cleanseth us from all sin." **1 John 1:7**

When we become one with the Lord, then we will be one with one another.

John 17:21-22 *says: "That they all may be one; as thou Father, art in me, and I in thee, that they also may be one in us: that the world may believe that thou hast sent me. And the Glory which thou gavest me, I have given them; that they may be one, even as we are one"*

God's reveals His Glory to those who walk in covenant with Him and that Glory makes us one! We must mature in the Love of God.

Perpetual Prayer and Worship

In the year 1727, there was a Christian Community led by a man named Count Nicolas Ludwig von Zinzendorf in Hernnhut, Germany. Initially when this community of 300 Moravian refugees was established, they faced many of the challenges that come with inter personal relationships. There were contentions, bickering and strife. But as they began to seek the Lord in prayer, worship and studying the Word of God together, God began to form them into a spiritual community. This, of course, is what brought unity among them. These are the ingredients of "covenant relationships". They became one in the Spirit because of their mutual communion with the Lord. It was not because of any affinity, or things they had in common or something one person had that would benefit another.

On August 13th, 1727 the Holy Spirit came down upon them in a powerful way. This was the fulfillment of a prophecy of revival given 100 years earlier. From this powerful visitation was born a perpetual twenty-four-hour a day, seven days a week, prayer and worship vigil that continued without ceasing for over 100 years!

The hearts of the Moravians began to burn with the things that were upon the heart of God. God gave them great vision and supernatural faith for their vision. They persisted, each generation, with a great passion and zeal. Their fire and spiritual hunger was contagious! They imparted it wherever they went.

Their hearts began to burn for lost souls and for the unreached peoples of the world. Over 200 dedicated missionaries were born and sent out to many nations. Such was the surrender of some of the missionaries; that they voluntarily sold themselves into slavery to be able to reach certain unreached groups.

This perpetual prayer and missionary movement, born in revival, marked one of the longest and purest moves of the Spirit in Church History and it radically changed the expression of Christianity.[11]

God is getting ready to do it again! In each generation down through the ages, God has always had His "Keepers of the Flame". They are a remnant who have loved, reverenced, protected, and carried the pure flame of the fire of the Holy Spirit. They have come through fire, through flood, through dangers and great persecutions. In the face of extreme situations, loving not their lives unto the death, in the good times and bad they have kept the flame and passed it to the next generation. Sometimes they were few and it seemed that the flame would die out. But there has always been a perpetual flame on the altar of God. So it shall be for the generations to come, perpetually, until the coming of the Lord!

It is time once again to PRAY without ceasing and call a solemn assembly. We must take the torch of the Fire of God for our generation and be "Keepers" of the Flame" in the midst of the dark days.

Exodus 30:7-9 *"And Aaron shall burn thereon sweet incense every morning: when he dresseth the lamps he shall burn incense upon it. And when Aaron lighteth the lamps at even, he shall burn incense upon it, a perpetual incense before the Lord throughout your generations."*

The Changing Landscape

A s we come more into these end-times it is vital that we come into a deeper walk in our Christian experience. This is a walk of exposing our own hearts and truly finding the heart of our Father God. We must know our God in love and intimacy. We must have an understanding of the times and God's ways. If we do not understand God's ways in this hour, we will be like a ship on a stormy sea without a sail or a compass. It will bring shipwreck in our lives.

The spiritual winds have shifted. Some continue on, as if nothing is happening. Some are in denial or totally unaware of what is up ahead. But many are standing at major crossroads in their lives. They are seeking direction. Some do not know where to turn, or how to proceed. Familiar landmarks of comfort zones are fading away. The very landscape is changing.

We must be alert to the call of Heaven to prepare our heart, life and ministry for complete change. It is time to evaluate the true values of life and eternity. At the beginning of the year, in a time of prayer, the Word of the Lord came forth: "Great change is coming, worship your way into it." Worship unlocks the door to the secret place and draws our hearts to the Lord's heart, and His heart to ours. *"Deep calleth unto deep . . ."* **Psalm 42:7**

Our Christian walk and ministry must be adequate to meet the extreme changes and situations that we will face. New challenges will arise. People's needs will change. Many powerful ministries may even find that, what has been successful in the past may not be adequate for the times that we are coming into. Only an encounter with the pure Glory of God will be adequate.

In this season, the outpouring of revival and ministries of power will not be determined by our spiritual gifting, or particular anointing. But it will be determined by where we have been in the Spirit. When I say "where we have been" I am not referring to churches, conferences or seminaries. But I am referring to Heavenly Places, Angelic Habitations, and personal Mount of Transfiguration experiences. We cannot take others where we have not been.

Our relationship with God must cease from being a knowledge of Him, from our human realm, and become a knowing Him, from His Holy realm. The Lord says: "It is time to cease from our outer court activity, and prepare our hearts for a Holy Place encounter".

Keys of the Kingdom

In this great season of change, God will begin to give fresh wisdom, revelation, and insight into the mysteries of God. In His wisdom, He will release Keys to the Kingdom to unlock needed truths to step into the uncharted territory ahead. His Word will begin to come alive with fresh revelation and layers of truth. These keys will include:

1. Keys of service, wisdom, understanding and insight into situations, and people's hearts and needs. New needs will present a demand for new answers.

2. Keys for fresh, keen discernment of spirits, and intent of the heart. This will be for our protection, as treachery and betrayal become more common both in the world and in the church.

3. Keys to walk in, and teach true holiness and repentance in an increasingly dark, depraved, and lawless environment. An environment, where even Christian culture, tolerance, ideals and morals are "evolving" before our very eyes. These values are far from the heart of the Christ of Christianity.

4. Keys to open doors to areas, regions, and nations that have seemed to be impenetrable and unreachable. In areas that have been closed to the Gospel for centuries, there will come great spiritual shifts over

entire nations. The light of Jesus Christ will penetrate where there has been great darkness and the final harvest will begin in an unprecedented magnitude.

5. Keys to high authority in higher intercession, and decreeing the Word of God and His will upon the earth. As the days become darker and more intense, our intercession will become more intense. There will be a need for greater intervention from God. Because of the need of the hour we must be able to contend for the faith in a new way.

6. Keys to worship, and the new song that will bring the atmosphere of heaven into our midst. God wants to release songs and melodies from heaven that will produce healing, miracles, signs and wonders. There will be new sounds of harmony and peace that will prepare us for the days ahead.

Worship will strengthen and prepare our soul to face the challenges ahead with faith and victory.

7. Keys of revival and the outpouring of the Holy Spirit that will introduce people to new aspects of God's Glory. We will see greater, deeply impacting encounters with the God of Glory, and the Glory of God that will mark our lives. We will also see a great increase in Angelic activity on our behalf .

A New Dispensation

We are noticeably stepping across a threshold of time. We are entering into a new dispensation, as is mentioned in **Ephesians 1:10** *"That in the dispensation of the fullness of times He might gather together in one all things in Christ, both which are in heaven and which are on earth; even in Him."* It is the dispensation of the fullness of times or what we call the "End-Times."

It is a time that we are crossing over from the "Church Age" to the "Kingdom Age" This is a time of great shift where we must shift our focus and priorities. The Lord is shifting our gaze heavenward. The storms and urgency of the hour will press us into this shift. In this shift, God is calling us from being "works" oriented, up to a higher place of habitation in His Manifest Presence.

God has given time to man in days, months and years, to live, to work and to serve Him, and make choices. But there is something very special about the time of a dispensation. In the old Webster Dictionary "dispensation" is defined as: "an increment of time, divinely orchestrated by God" That tells me that if this set time is divinely orchestrated by God, then God is in control! It also tells me that it is a sovereign season. It is a time marked, established and set in motion by God. Neither man nor devil nor the gates of hell themselves shall be able to alter what God has ordained to come to pass in this hour. The enemy may try to force his hand or try and pre-empt God's plan, but he cannot. The best thing that we can do, is to align ourselves with God's heart and times. It is time to fully surrender, set our sail and flow with God. When we cease from our own plans and works, and surrender to God's, He will lift us up into a higher dimension of His Glory. From this Glory we will begin to see these end-time events unfold from a whole new perspective. This is the place of ". . . *A thousand shall fall at thy side, and ten thousand at thy right hand, but it shall not come nigh thee."* **Psalm 91:7**

Yes, the enemy does have his timetable of events for these end-times. These events have been covertly planned for many years and are being set in motion. These events seem to be advancing and unfolding on the world at an alarming rate. While fear and uncertainty permeate the air, they seek to dominate the hearts and minds of God's people. This is where we must allow God to shift our perspective from fact to truth and from fear to faith.

95

It is a FACT that stress and turmoil will increase as the confrontation between light and darkness intensifies, but it is TRUE that God remains on His Throne. God also has a plan and a set timetable of events. Even as the enemy has decreed a thing, God has also decreed a thing. He shall bring it to pass and *". . .The earth shall be full of the knowledge of the Lord, as the waters cover the sea."* **Isaiah 11:9**

*"Where darkness and sin abound, grace will much more abound"***Romans 5:20**

Yes, it is important to be aware of this present darkness and the hour that we live in. But, we must also have a clear vision of God's promise of His Glory for this hour, and this generation. These are the best of times and the worst of times. It is certainly not a time to lower our arms in defeat and discouragement. Many times we fail in the little things of temperament and attitudes etc. But times of crisis show us what we really are, as we take courage, and evaluate the true values of life and eternity. This is the hour that we were born for! Keep your eyes on the goal and your heart at the Throne.

The Five Hundred Year Phenomena

God has created and orchestrated the universe with such an intricate, precise intelligent design. Everything flows together in it's course, rhythm and time like a fine tuned Swiss watch but on a much grander scale.

The words to the song "indescribable" by Chris Tomlin say it all:

"From the highest of heights to the depth of the sea,
Creation revealing Your Majesty.
From the colors of fall to the fragrance of spring,
Every creature unique in the song that he sings.
All exclaiming, indescribable, uncontainable,
You placed the stars in the sky and you know them by name.
You are amazing God!
All powerful, untamable,
Awestruck we fall to our knees as we humbly proclaim.
You are amazing God!
Who has told every lightening bolt where it should go?
Or see heavenly storehouses laden with snow?
Who imagined the sun and gave source to it's light?
Yet conceals it to bring us the coolness of night?
None can fathom. Incomparable, unchangeable,
You see the depth of my heart and you love me the same.
You are amazing God![12]

Psalms 8:34 *says: "When I consider the heavens, the work of thy fingers, the moon and the stars which* *thou hast ordained. What is man that Thou art mindful of him?"*

God has set the heavens in their course. Every sun, moon and star has it's own brilliance and a song that they sing giving glory to God their Creator.

Even as we spoke earlier in this book about the cycles of our soul, we see that the entire universe is set on cycles. The solar cycles, lunar cycles, spring, summer, winter, fall, seed time and harvest, even the cycles of birth, life and death. Everything has a course of time as it says in **Ecclesiastes 3:1-8** *"To everything there is a season and a time to every purpose under heaven. . . ."*

There are marked times in history that have been patterned by shifts and changes of great magnitude. These shifts and changes have affected entire climates, nations, cultures, civilizations and religions. There is a consistent 500 year pattern that has been traced through history. The 500 year phenomena is a cyclic pattern that can be traced back to when God spoke to Noah to build the Ark and the great flood that ensued. Every 500 years thereafter has brought more great shifts and changes. The 500 year marks in history are as follows:

1. The Davidic Dynasty: The rise and rule of King David and his descendants from 970 BC

2. The Babylonian Captivity: The exile of the Jews from the ancient kingdom of Judah in 597 BC

3. The Great Transformation: The beginning of Christianity's religious traditions in 49 AD

4. The Fall of Rome and the Council of Chalcedon: The fourth Ecumenical Council. It's purpose was to assert Catholic doctrine against the heresies of Eutyches from 451 – 481 AD

5. The Great Schism and the Crusades: The Great Schism divided the Western Catholic world from the Eastern Orthodox world. The Crusades to the Holy Land and against Islam also had a great impact on the then known world began in 1051 AD

6. The Great Reformation: which began with Martin Luther and the 95 thesis. The beginning of the Protestant Movement in 1517AD

7. Now:–The dawn of a new day, another 500 year shift.[13]

In studying these dates we can see that in each of these 500 year shifts, there was an overlap time of anywhere from 8 to 73 years. This indicates that these significant shifts were not immediate events that suddenly occurred in one day. But these shifts or events were set in motion and were completed in a season of time. This will also be the progression in this season that we are in. Some major shifts have already been set in motion.

As On the Day of Creation

There is another incredible God orchestrated cyclic phenomena regarding the 28 year solar cycle that is recorded in ancient Jewish writings. This once again proves the magnificence of God's intricate plan regarding man and His power to intervene in times of great crisis.

"What is man, that Thou are mindful of him" **Psalm 8:4**

Once every 28 years the Jews commemorate the fact that the sun is once again in the exact position as it was on the day of creation. This always takes place in the Jewish calendar month of Nisan or the western calendar month of April. IT HAPPENED JUST IN 2009!

Only once every 532 years does this solar cycle begin on the same day of the month as at creation. IT HAPPENED JUST IN 2009!

Only 3 times before in 6,000 years has it taken place on the 14th of Nisan which is Passover. IT HAPPENED JUST IN 2009!

Each of these times was directly followed by great miracles and mighty interventions from God.

1. The first time was the Great Exodus from Egypt when God parted the Red Sea and the children of Israel passed over on dry ground and Pharoah's armies were destroyed. **Exodus 13:17-22**

2. The second time was when the Jews were in peril of annihilation because of wicked Hamen. Queen Esther fasted and came before the king on behalf of her people. The Jews were spared. **Esther 3:6-8:14**

3. The third time was at the Cross when Jesus was crucified or what the Jews know as the rending of the veil of the Temple from top to bottom.[14] **Matthew 27: 32-51**

At these crucial moments in history of such great change, we can either go into a new cycle of blessing and positive change or we can be thrown into a dark, destructive cycle. In time of crisis we must rise up in courage and raise the standard spiritually by our prayers but also by our voice and by our actions! We must PRAY that the wrong history does not repeat itself.

We stand once again at a mighty crossroads in God's history when we desperately need a mighty intervention of God in the midst of the darkness of storm and impending danger. We can look up with a steadfast hope knowing that our redemption draweth nigh.

In Luke chapter 21 it speaks of the end-time events that shall come to pass. **Luke 21:26b-28** *says: "for the powers of heaven shall be shaken and then shall they see the Son of man coming in a cloud with power and great glory. And when these things begin to come to pass, then look up and lift up your heads; for your redemption draweth nigh".*

God has done it before and He will do it again! We were born for such a time as this!

"The Avante – Garde"

It is always in crucial times of major change like these in history that God raises up a special people, "born out of time" as it were. They have a prophetic sense of the times. I call them the Avante-Garde or the Vanguard.

The definition of Vanguard is: a part of an army that go ahead of the main troops to "spy out the land". They also are those who lead reformation movements. These movements can be literary, artistic, political, or spiritual.

The Vanguard will always have ideas that contrast traditional ones.

1. They are ahead leading the way for change.

2. They are always the first to see, and the first to move.

3. They are not afraid to take risks, or steps of introduction, even though it may mean opposition, persecution or misunderstanding.

4. They have an understanding of the times and what is needed to bring change.

5. They lift the standard spiritually to usher in change.

6. They are visionaries and revolutionaries.

God prepares and raises up the Vanguard:

1. In times of crisis and troubled times.

2. When people's hearts are far from God and their vision dim.

3. In times of idolatry and spiritual mixture.

4. In times of spiritual transition that will mark history.

This certainly does describe the times that we are living in. We know that there are storms on the horizon of a magnitude of what we have not faced in our lifetime. It is definitely an hour when God is raising up His special breed of deliverers.

Esther – A Deliverer in Her Day

God is getting ready to raise up deliverers, out of obscurity, from among those who have been in their secret chambers, being prepared in the "beauty of holiness" with sweet oils of purification.

These deliverers will begin to emerge, seemingly coming out of nowhere. They are a remnant of the nameless, fameless generation. It will be a surprise to many. They will say: "Who is this?", What is their name?", "Where did they come from?" They will emerge prepared for this hour to take their God given place. These are "hidden saints", who have been in the secret place of communion with the Lord. They have not sought for recognition or wealth or fame but are well known before the Throne of God. They are those who have been quietly loving and worshipping Him, quietly weeping and interceding for others, quietly living a holy life and walking the love walk, quietly making a difference, wherever they go. They have learned an understanding of God, and His ways by walking with Him.

"Who is this that cometh up from the wilderness, leaning upon her beloved? **Song of Solomon 8:5a**

Esther is a type of the Bride of Christ, who is coming into her finest hour. This is our time of great purpose. We truly are "born for such a time as this."

Esther 2:12 *"Now when every maids' turn was come to go in to King Ahasuerus, after that she has been twelve months, according to the manner of the women, (for so were the days of their purification accomplished, to wit, six months with oil of myrrh and six months with sweet odors, and with other things for the purifying of the women;)*

The following portion was inspired by notes taken from a sermon I heard preached in Jerusalem in 2007 by a prophet of God, Robert Stearns, who is one of the clearest prophetic voices I know of for this hour.[15]

Esther found great favor in the eyes of the king. It was Esther's beauty and sincere heart, that caused her to find favor with the king. It wasn't any qualifications of wealth, position, family background or connections, that brought her to that place. Only the favor and Divine Destiny of God could do that.

Actually Esther had three strikes against her that would seemingly disqualify her from greatness:

1. She was an orphan in a dysfunctional situation, who had not known the nurture of a mother's love.

2. She was a woman, in a man's world. Women, in those days, and in that culture had very limited options as to what their lives would be. Actually, her only option was to become a wife, but she had no dowry.

3. She was a Jew. It was very unwise and unsafe to make that known at that time, as it could have meant her life.

Thanks be to God that He does not determine our future by our past!

Not long after Esther's entrance into the palace, amid all the beauty, splendor and comfort, great trouble arose in the land. Esther had become "familiar" with her new life and she forgot that her position was unto purpose and not just for the benefits thereof.

Mordecai was desperately trying to get the message to Esther, in the midst of her busyness, of the urgent storm that was arising. Wicked Haman was plotting to annihilate the Jewish people. **Esther 4:11-16**

At first Esther was looking for someone else to answer the call. "Surely there is someone who will "wake-up" and answer the call and save us!"

If we, the Bride, do not hear the wake-up call and speak up, in this hour, is there **anyone** that will?

There are three things that can deafen our ears to the cry of the Spirit:

1. Distraction: being too busy with "things". Even ministry can get in the way of purpose.

2. Denial: Esther did not want to accept that things could be as bad as they were.

3. Comfort and ease: "Don't rock the boat!" Don't shake my world!"

When Esther finally "heard" the urgent plea, she became alert and active. She called a fast and reckoned the price that she may have to pay for action. "If I perish, I perish" **Esther 4:16**

Awake, Bride of Christ! Before it is too late!

When Esther did awaken:

1. She recognized the reality of the situation and no longer allowed denial and comfort to shield her from reality.

2. Esther cried unto the Lord! She did not call a counsel of the Royal Court, or check their military strength. She called a corporate fast.

3. She took a risk in the face of great danger and said: "If I perish, I perish".

God is preparing us in these crucial days to "love not our lives unto the death" but to love Him more. If your cause is not worth dying for, it is not worth living for.

Revelation 12:11 *"and they overcame him (the devil) by the blood of the Lamb and by the word of their testimony; and they loved not their lives unto the death."*

4. In the time of great crisis Esther took courage and arose to the occasion. We need to have courage in this hour to make the, right, Godly, decisions and take the actions we must take.[15]

It is said that courage is not a decision of the will but it is a moral virtue. It comes from the strength of the Spirit. Crisis will bring out moral virtues in some, but in others it will reveal hidden weakness. That is why these will be days of treachery and betrayal but also days of great exploits.

Those Who Know Their God

Daniel 11:32b *"the people that do know their God shall be strong and do exploits."*

Those who know their God shall do exploits. That is the key in this hour. We must know our God. Not know about Him but really KNOW Him, intimately. We must know His heartbeat. He has a heartbeat for this time in history, and for our lives. In that heartbeat, is every answer that we need, to effect great and positive change. We are not a people abandoned to be victims of fate, "come what may". But we are of the people most privileged and blessed on earth. We stand at the threshold of one of the greatest opportunities since the beginning of time, right before us. Do you have your finger on God's pulse? Can you feel His heartbeat? Do you need to move in a little closer? Do you need to get quiet and listen a little more intently?

God desires to raise up a generation of deliverers once again. He must raise up a people of deliverance once again with a strong voice of authority to call His people back to their first Love. This is a call to turn our hearts and faces heavenward with a renewed love and surrender. This is a call to turn again to the paths of righteousness, truth, and holiness. This is the only path that will lead us through the coming storm to a greater day. The church must repent, and turn from her wicked ways. As goes the church, so goes the nation.

"If my people which are called by My name shall humble themselves and pray and seek My face, and turn from THEIR wicked ways; then will I hear from heaven, and will forgive their sin and will heal their land." **II Chronicles 7:14**

God is not addressing the non believer here. He is speaking of His people. It is easy to try and analyze the reasons why systems fail and things crumble around us. We blame people, policies, governments and economy. When God's Hand of blessing and protection lifts, things change. People do not crumble in a day. Nations do not crumble in a day.

All through the word of God it shows the rise and fall of kingdoms, nations, and people. The pattern is always the same. When they did things God's way, and obeyed His commands, and placed Him as Sovereign King over them, the people and the nation prospered and were blessed. When they took matters into their own hands and did not honor God, His hand of blessing and protection lifted. God's people suffered and kingdoms fell.

It is time to come clean, and be brutally honest with ourselves and with God. Call things just as they are. Do not make excuses, and reason, and justify sin, just repent! It is only as God lifts the standard spiritually in us, that we can be used of God to lift the standard around us. May God restore to His Church the POWER and AUTHORITY, to rule and reign in heavenly places, with Christ Jesus, over the wicked principalities that are seeking to destroy the nations and the people of the earth. True, Godly power and authority operate and are released by a higher standard.

Psalm 24:3-6 *"Who shall ascend the hill of the Lord? Who shall stand in His Holy place? He that hath clean hands and a pure heart: who hath not lifted up his soul unto vanity, nor sworn deceitfully. He shall receive the blessing from the Lord and* *righteousness from the God of His salvation. This is the generation of them that seek His face."*

The Hour of Judgment

When many hear of "God's Judgment" they tend to look upon it with fear, dread, uncertainty, and resistance. Some well meaning Christians even say that it doesn't exist. They call it a gloom and doom message that is not relevant for New Testament believers.

Psalm 19:9 *"The fear of the Lord is clean, enduring forever: the judgments of the Lord, are true and righteous altogether."*

We can clearly see from Scripture, that God's judgment is just as much a part of His character, as is His love and holiness It is just an aspect of His character that we are not accustomed to seeing. If it were not for His standard of love and holiness, there would be no need for His judgment. Because He is a loving, holy and just God, there must be a plumb line of truth to uphold His standard. This is the judgment of God.

Daniel 12:9-10 *shares a mystery about God's end-time judgment: ". . . Go thy way Daniel; for the words are closed up and sealed till the time of the end. Many shall be purified and made white and tried; but the wicked shall do wickedly; and none of the wicked shall understand, but the wise shall understand."*

As we look at the Hebrew and Greek for the word "judgment", we see that for the wicked it is a sentence, a condemnation, a punishment, a verdict and a scourge. But for the righteous it can be justice, mercy, vindication, avenging and defense.

It is only as the plumb line of God's truth and holiness falls upon the secret place of our heart, that it will determine what part of God's judgment will be our portion. Remember that even God's judgments are based on His mercy.

"In Time of Judgment Stay Under The Blood"

Exodus 12:12-13 *"For I will pass through the land of Egypt this night and will smite all the firstborn in the land of Egypt, both man and beast; and against all the gods of Egypt I will execute judgment: I am the Lord. And the blood shall be to you for a token upon the houses where you are: and when I see the* *blood, I will pass over you, and the plague shall not be upon you to destroy you, when I smite the land of Egypt."*

In this scripture we see that this time called "Passover", was a time of swift judgment in the land of Egypt, and against their gods. The Lord had decreed that the death angel would pass through the land, to take all the firstborn in the land. This was the firstborn of every house (adult and child) and the firstborn of every beast. It was a very dark night, both naturally, and spiritually, and in the hearts of men.

In the midst of the imminent darkness, God spoke to His people and gave them a great provision for their protection. It was the blood of the lamb upon the doorposts of their homes. The Lord said: "When I see the blood, I will pass over thee". We have the same provision today through the Blood of the Lamb, Jesus Christ.

It is very important, in these dark times, we stay under the Blood of Jesus. Keep short accounts with others and with God. Apply the Blood of Jesus daily to you and your house. You shall see the salvation of your God in the time of judgment.

Psalm 91;5-8 *"Thou shalt not be afraid for the terror by night, nor the arrow that flieth by day, nor for the pestilence that walketh in darkness, nor for the destruction that wasteth at noonday. A thousand shall fall at thy side and ten thousand at thy right hand but* *it shall not come nigh thee. Only with thine eyes shalt thou behold and see the reward of the wicked."*

The gavel has been lowered in the courts of Heaven. God has set in motion His decrees for Glory and for judgment. We must understand that when we begin to see God's judgment come, it is a sign to us that His Glory is imminent. When we see evil brought to light, when greed and corruption are exposed, when innocent blood is avenged, then we know to look up, for God's Glory is on the horizon. Because where there is delayed judgment, there is an absence of glory. But where the Glory of God is present there is immediate judgment. Also, the longer He puts off His judgment, the greater it will be when it comes.

Ananias and Sapphira

We see an account of immediate judgment in the early church in **Acts 5:1-11.** *"But a certain man named Ananias, with Sapphira, his wife, sold a possession. And kept back part of the price, his wife also being privy to it, and brought a certain part and laid it at the Apostles feet. But Peter said, Ananias, why has satan filled thy heart to lie to the Holy Ghost, and to keep back part of the price of the land? Whiles it remained, was it not thine own? And after it was sold was it not in thine own power? Why hast thou conceived this thing in thine*

116

heart? Thou hast not lied unto men, but unto God. And Ananias hearing these words fell down and gave up the ghost: and great fear came on all them that heard these things. And, the young men arose, wound him up, and carried him out, and buried him. And it was about the space of three hours after, when his wife, not knowing what was done, came in. And Peter answered unto her, tell me whether thou sold the land for so much? And she said, yea, for so much. Then Peter said unto her, how is it that ye have agreed together to tempt the spirit of the Lord? Behold the feet of them which have buried thy husband are at the door, and shall carry thee out. Then fell she down straightway at his feet, and yielded up the ghost: and the young men came in, and found her dead, and carried her forth and buried her by her husband. And great fear came upon all the church, and upon as many as heard these things."

It was a time when the Glory of God was in their midst, and many "signs and wonders" were being wrought by the hands of the Apostles. Ananias and Sapphira agreed together to lie to the Holy Ghost. They thought that they had only lied to man, and that it would be their secret. They appeared to give all, in the eyes of men. All the while, lying to a Holy God, who searches the hearts, and knows, what is the mind of the Spirit. **Romans 8:27a**

It says that great fear fell upon the church, and on all who heard these things. This was a "sign and wonder", that God's Glory was in their midst. The

117

church of Acts was a church that walked in the Fear of the Lord. This was a source of great power. Oh, how we need the Fear of the Lord restored in the church today! Because we have lost the Fear of the Lord, we have lost moral values and the conviction of sin, thus we have lost the gift of true repentance. When we lose the Fear of the Lord, we begin to justify our motives and actions, instead of repent of them.

The Manifest Fear of the Lord

A couple of years ago, I was ministering in a nation that had once experienced tremendous revival for many years. I had the privilege of ministering there many times, in the "heat" of the revival. During that season churches were working together in unity. There was a tremendous hunger for the Word of God, and for the Presence of the Lord. Healings, deliverances and signs and wonders were abundant. Literally, millions came into the Kingdom during that time. It truly was a modern day phenomena of God that shook a nation.

As the years went by, the move of the Holy Spirit continued in such a way that most would only dream of. Churches were prospering, but many began to become "familiar" with the Presence of the Lord. There wasn't that reverence that was once there. Pastors, that had worked together, were parting ways. Leaders were falling into sexual sins, and were being tempted with finances. The church nationwide was hearing of these things and was being profoundly affected.

I was very grieved at what was happening, and I began to seek the Lord earnestly as to what would be the "Word of the Lord", for that season and that people. He began to speak to me about the "Fear of the Lord".

One evening in the middle of a sermon on the Fear of the Lord, the manifest Fear of the Lord literally began to fill the church. There were 12 of the worship team that stayed on the platform behind me as I ministered. I began to hear a weeping and an intense sobbing behind me at my feet. The entire worship team was on their face before the Lord. People were kneeling at their seats and some were making their way to the altar. A great weeping and repentance broke out. There had been no altar call. I hadn't even finished the message. It was a sovereign move of the Holy Spirit. That's the way I like it. The Holy Spirit can interrupt any time He wants to!

II Corinthians 7:1 *says that "Holiness is perfected by the Fear of the Lord". Holiness, purity, and the Fear of the Lord, go hand in hand. You cannot know one without the other. These are all worked out in our lives, only by an intimate relationship, and passion for the Lord.*

It is the Fear of the Lord that will keep us in the ways of the Lord. It will keep us walking circumspectly before Him.

If we love God and are right with Him, this kind of "fear" is not one that would cause us to cower from the Lord, nor seek to want to run from His Presence. It is a Holy Fear, that stands in awe of the greatness, and majesty of a Holy, Loving, All powerful, Creator God. It is a worshipful fear, birthed out of great love and respect. It is a reverence, honor and veneration of this Mighty King, who rules over our lives, and the universe. It is a knowing that there is not a thought, nor a deed, that escapes His gaze.

The original Hebrew and Greek define the Fear of the Lord as: reverence, honor, veneration, awe, and dread.

There are many powerful promises throughout the Word of God for those who fear the Lord. The following are just a few, that we must hold in our heart, that are keys for the days that we are coming into.

Deuteronomy 6:24 *"And the Lord commanded us to do all these statutes, to fear the Lord our God, for our good always, that He might preserve us alive, as it is at this day."*

Psalm 33:18-19 *"Behold the eye of the Lord is upon them that fear Him, upon them that hope in His mercy. To deliver their soul from death and to keep them alive in famine."*

Psalm 34:7 *"The Angel of the Lord encampeth around about them that fear Him, and delivereth them."*

Psalm 31:19-20 *"Oh how great is Thy goodness, which Thou hast laid up for them that fear Thee; which Thou hast wrought for them that trust in Thee before the sons of men! Thou shalt hide them in the secret of Thy presence from the pride of man: Thou shalt keep them secretly in a pavilion from the strife of tongues."*

Psalms 25:14 *"The secret of the Lord is with them that fear Him; and He will shew them His covenant."*

The Fear of the Lord is a vital part of "Secret Place" abiding and of knowing God's favor and open heaven over our lives. When we encounter and embrace the Fear of the Lord, as a part of our life, and spiritual worship, it will transform our lives. It will be a divine restraint upon our lives, that will govern our thoughts, actions and decisions. Explicit obedience is a fruit of the Fear of the Lord.

When we lack the Fear of the Lord, we will fear man. We will serve whom or what we fear. It is the Fear of the Lord that will keep us from sin, and lawlessness, but, it is the Love of God that will keep us from legalism. The Fear of the Lord is our wisdom. **Job 28:28** *". . .Behold, the Fear of the Lord, that is wisdom; and to depart from evil is understanding."*

The Mantle of Holiness and Repentance

There is a lot of acclaim that comes with the ministry of signs, wonders and miracles. But yet one of the most rare and little seen mantles of anointing today, is an anointing that brings men to repentance. No amount of fervent preaching, singing or ministry gifts will produce true repentance, unless it is under the mantle of Holiness, Purity and the Fear of the Lord. This kind of mantle is only found in "Secret Place" abiding. It is imparted as we stay in the fervency of intimate communion with the Lord, and beholding Him in the beauty of His Holiness.

Perhaps, Charles Finney, a powerful evangelist from the mid to late 1800's carried the greatest and most fiery mantle of Holiness, Purity and the Fear of the Lord that the world has known in the last 150 years. He could walk into a building and stand silent. Just the atmosphere that he carried spoke louder and more penetrating than any words. People would begin to weep and repent, acknowledging their need for God. He actually had an open heaven or "heavenly portal" over his life that had a sphere of a sixty mile radius! This is saying, that within a sixty mile radius of where Charles Finney was preparing to enter a town, the conviction of sin, and the Fear of the Lord would begin to fall upon the people. It would fall in their homes, schools, business' and in the streets. Travel was much slower in those days, so instead of a one hour journey, it could take as much as two to three days. So for two to three days before Finney arrived, that sixty mile sphere of "heavenly portal" was moving ahead of him, changing the atmosphere and preparing the hearts of the people. It was the influence of the Holy Spirit preparing the way to shake a city![16]

This mantle is a tangible element of God's Power and Glory, which He is restoring and manifesting, in this hour, to bring in the great end-time harvest of souls, who are awaiting the wind of the Spirit to blow upon them. It will be a sovereign sweeping of Glory over the ripened, harvest fields of the nations!

The Secret Place of the Most High

It says in **Psalm 18:11:** *"He (God) made darkness His secret place; his pavilion round about him were dark waters and thick clouds of the skies."*

We know that the eminence of God is pure light. The Scripture says here that He has chosen to make darkness His secret place. In this, we see, that even thick darkness is not void of God, for He dwells in the darkness. So no matter how much evil seems to be pervading and how dark the circumstance, God is in the midst. He is not far away. He is right there, just a call away. He is hidden in the darkness, just beyond a thin veil, waiting for us to call upon Him and seek Him out, and He will say: "Here am I". By the Spirit, we can slip the bonds of earth, where from this side we see only darkness, and step into the pure light of God. Even though we remain in the same situation, we can be clothed in light and see through the eyes of light. This is the paradox of the natural realm and spiritual realm running parallel. The realm of God is just a thin veil away.

The Power of Abiding in the Secret Place: There is a powerful canopy of protection and favor that comes over our life when we abide in the Secret Place, that will take us through everything we may have to face in life. When we go through emotional turmoil, hate, fear, confusion, and strife, God's canopy of protection can cover us, so that the fiery darts of the enemy do not harm our soul nor get into our spirit.

Psalm 31:20 *says: "Thou shalt hide them in the secret of thy presence from the pride of man: thou shalt keep them secretly in a pavilion from the strife of tongues."*

And in **Psalm 27:4-5** *it says: "One thing have I desired of the Lord, that will I seek after; that I may dwell in the house of the Lord all the days of my life, to behold the beauty of the Lord, and to enquire in His Temple. For in the time of trouble he shall hide me in his pavilion: in the secret of his tabernacle he shall hide me; he shall set me up upon a rock".*

While we are busy beholding the beauty of the Lord, and adoring Him, He is covering us with a canopy of His Love and protection. What a wonderful arrangement!

Even in the most dangerous or severe situations, God is there, covering our soul. His protection includes bodily protection. Although, there are special elect ones, who have been called to walk the walk of extreme suffering or martyrdom. Even then the Grace and Love of God is there to cover them.

It says of Stephen in the hour of his persecution, and martyrdom that he was: *"full of the Holy Ghost , looked up steadfastly into heaven, and saw the glory of God, and Jesus standing at the right hand of God, and said, behold I see the heavens opened, and the son of man standing on the right hand of God"*. **Acts 7:55-56**

I envision Stephen being enveloped in a brilliant cloud of God's Glory at that moment, in such a way that he did not feel the pain of his stoning. His spirit was "caught up" in that same Glory when He died. At that given moment, if we walk in love and forgiveness, God will give us, a divine release from all earthly bonds and struggles. There is a mighty grace available when we are called to go through great suffering or even death. When we have that resolve and fire of His love in our hearts to "love not our lives unto the death", we can then say; "if I perish, I perish". Before we can know the abundance of life, and freedom of total abandon, in serving Christ, we must come to this resolve, of being willing to lose our life for the sake of Christ.

I once read a testimony of a pastor, who suffered 20 years in a lonely prison cell, in communist

Russia, in almost total solitary confinement. He was completely separated from family and friends or even news of their wellbeing. At night, he had just a thin, straw mattress on the floor, that he was allowed to sleep on, for just a few hours, but for the rest of the time he had to just stand and walk circles in his cell. There was nowhere to sit or rest. If he did weaken or falter, he was beaten unmercifully. At the end of the twenty years, he was sent to a Siberian hard labor camp, for another four years. Even in the midst of the extreme treatment, cruelty, and suffering, the fire and love of God continued to burn bright in his heart. He had no bitterness nor anger in his heart. He truly was a "Keeper of the Flame". Many of us will probably not have to face extreme suffering but some will. Do we have the fire of God's love in our hearts in such a way that it would sustain us through such extreme suffering?[17]

A Call to the Bride to Come into Your Inheritance:

There is a higher place, a higher dimension, that the Lord is calling His Bride to "step up", "reach up" and "come up" to. It is a higher place of abiding that is prepared and reserved for you. It has been planned in the heart of God throughout the ions of time. It is your inheritance for this hour. That in this hour, the hour of the fullness of time, the veil of revelation shall be rent, and the mysteries of God shall be revealed to you. This is reserved for His beloved who follow hard after Him and fear His name.

Isaiah 45:3 *"And I will give thee the treasures of darkness and hidden riches of secret places, that thou mayest know that I, the Lord, which call thee by thy name, am the God of Israel."*

This is a place of wholly abiding, in a consummate relationship, nurtured by an intense, holy, love, that conquers our soul. This place shall become our home, where we go no more out from His Presence, but learn to dwell, and live, and carry this Holy Atmosphere of Heaven.

This is the heartbeat of the prophetic call of this book and the heart of God for this season.

The Lord says: It is time to draw aside and *"Be still and know that I am God"* **Psalm 46:10**

The Lord is looking for those that are standing at attention, with their gaze focused heavenward. He is looking for those whom He can call up into the secret counsels of heaven, to receive fresh wisdom, and understanding. God wants to give us a clarity of vision and purpose for this hour. He wants to pour out the realms of His Glory for these end-times. He wants to pour the intensity of His Glory upon our countenance.

Abiding in The Secret Place

Let us take a closer look at the word "dwelleth" in **Psalm 91:1.** The Hebrew origin says the following:

The word "**dwelleth**" means to sit down with, tarry, remain with, continue with, to establish a habitation, return to, keep house with, live with, cohabit together, change residence.

God did not create us as independent beings to carry a concept of God according to what our belief system will allow. Religion does this. It has no life giving force or source. It is just a *"form of godliness denying the power thereof"* **11 Timothy 3:5.**

God has created us for full union with Him, to give us full revelation and full access, to all that Heaven offers.

When Jesus said "come follow me", He wasn't suggesting we follow Him at a distance, or when it was convenient. He was asking, will you truly follow Me? Will you walk with Me? Will you study My ways up close and learn of them? Will you walk with Me, in such a way, that you will really come to know Me and be able to anticipate My steps, My words and My desires? This is true love.

When the Lord makes this call to us to dwell in His Secret Place, to abide with Him, in His Holy habitation, it is not to come in and go out on temporary visit, at our choosing, or convenience. This is a call to the Bride, for covenant relationship. It is a union of love and purpose.

He is asking, will you abide and continue with Me? Will you make My presence and will your priority and hearts desire? Can you make the transition to make My heart your home? Will you have all that you do spring forth from here? In essence, He is saying to His bride; "will you marry Me?" "Will you make Me your chief desire and center of your life?" "May my Secret Chamber be your home?"

It is time for the Bride to change residence! It is time to say good-bye to this old house of fear, worry, loneliness and lack, and come into the abundance of our full inheritance in the "Secret Place of the Most High!

As you hear the call of the Spirit to "come up higher", may God's Heavenly Portal be opened to you, to know the fullness of the power of abiding in the "Secret Place" in these End-Times".

End Notes

1. Barna Research Group
   www.soundthealarm.net/barnapollmillions-
   leavingtraditionalchurch.html

2. For more information on the soul read "Latent
   Power of the Soul" by Watchman Nee

3. Information on metamorphosis of the Monarch
   Butterfly
   www.monarch-butterfly.com/monarch-butter-
   flies-facts.html

4. Information on "sincere" vessels, pottery.
   www.yrm.org/sincerity.htm

5. Information on communication verbal / non-
   verbal.
   www.hodu.com/louder.shtml#7c

6. More information on Ministering Angels read: "Our Ministering Angels" by Gwen R. Shaw, available from Engeltal Press, #1-870-446-2665, www.EngeltalPress.com

7. More information on Seasonal and Ancient Portals, read "The Ancient Portals of Heaven" by David Herzog, published by Destiny Image. www.destinyimage.com

8. Eagles in a storm: www.indianchild.com/eagles_in_a_storm.htm

9. "Eye of the Storm" en.wikipedia.org/wiki/eye_ (cyclone)

10. 5 steps for practical preparation: "The Perfect Storm" by John Paul Jackson. Youtube.com (31 minute video clip) WSTK-ITV – AWE TV

11. Hernnhut Germany Christian Community 1727. www.thewellumc.com

12. Lyrics to song by Chris Tomlin "Indescribable" www.lyricsmode.com/lyrics/c/chris_tomlin/indescribable.html

13. Information on the 500 year phenomena www.thegreatemergence.com (2 minute 45 second video clip)

14. Day of creation, more information on: "The Blessing of the Sun" (Birchat HaChama) www.betemunah.org/hachama.html by, Hillel Ben David (Greg Killian)

15. Points made from notes taken from a sermon preached by Robert Stearns in 2007 in Jerusalem. For more in depth, timely information on this subject, read: "The Cry of Mordecai" By Robert Stearns published by Destiny Image www.destinyimage.com

16. More information on Charles Finney and his works: www.charlesfinney.com (public domain)

17. More information on the persecuted church: The Voice of the Martyrs "Extreme Devotion" by Thomas Nelson Publishing

Breinigsville, PA USA
11 June 2010
239705BV00002B/2/P